HAS 'WASHINGTON' LEGS? & DINGO

TWO PLAYS BY

CHARLES WOOD

A Methuen New Theatrescript
Eyre Methuen · London

First published in Great Britain in 1978 by Eyre Methuen Ltd,
11 New Fetter Lane, London EC4P 4EE

Printed in Great Britain by Expression Printers Ltd, London

ISBN 0 413 34040 6

HAS 'WASHINGTON' LEGS?

Has 'Washington' Legs? was first staged by the National Theatre in the Cottesloe on November 29 1978. The cast was as follows:

THE AMERICANS	
JOE VERIATO	Bob Hoskins
WESLEY	Gawn Grainger
SY HOELMERSBAGGER	Lionel Murton
DANIEL RASHUR	Richard Perkins
CARL DORF	Niall Toibin
MICKEY BOORMAN	Derek Thompson
PAT SLIGO	Martin Howells
JOHN BEAN	Albert Finney
JOHN D'ORSAY	Alexander Allenby
MARY JANE PENDEJO	Tel Stevens
THE ENGLISH	
SIR FLUTE PARSONS	Robert Stephens
MAURICE	Timothy Block
RED LEAD	Frederick Warder
ELF	Brian Clover
BERNIE THE VOLT	Peter Armitage
CAMEL	Martin Howells
BIRDIE	Norman Tyrrell
FLIM	James Grant
POOH BEAR	Keith Skinner
CLAW	Adam Norton
HEINRICH GUTTMEIR	Peter Jolley
ONE ABSOLUTELY AUTHENTIC BRITISH SOLDIER	Ray Edwards
Director	Geoffrey Reeves
Settings	William Dudley
Costumes	Pamela Howard

ACT ONE

The Scene: The south bank of the river Thames in London, England, circa 1976.

1 The Curtain rises

On wet concrete,
shining whiter than white concrete,
great silver/grey/white slabs of it,
towering and looming and jutting out
over chairs of plastic and steel on
thick pile carpet of brown wool; and
in the centre of the cluster of
chairs, a glass table with tubular
steel legs, low and lit by shafts of
yellow, sometimes sun and sometimes
electric which leaks and dribbles
and stingingly spurts under and round
and about the ramps, bulwarks,
bastions, bagnoires, boulevards,
battlements, bocages, twinkles in the
Sony eyes of concrete boats, searches
and sweeps, picks and rummages into
and under everything laid on the slabs
or festering in the cracks, cowering
in the seeming dark of the cantilevering,
swooping overhead on cranes.

Or, alternatively: an empty stage.

In every Sony eye on every concrete
prow, a flicker of black and white
and sound of voices talking, talking,
talking one to the other, one on top
of the other, the voices of HUMPHREY
BOGART, GEORGE RAFT, LAUREN
BACALL, GARY COOPER, JAMES
CAGNEY, SPENCER TRACY,
MAXINE COOPER, KATHARINE
HEPBURN, PETER LORRE,
CAROLE LOMBARD, WILLIAM
BENDIX, CLARK GABLE, PAULINE
GODDARD, MAXINE COOPER,
HUMPHREY BOGART, GEORGE
RAFT, RONALD REAGAN, BRIAN
DONLEVY, JACK LA RUE, PAUL
MUNI, HUMPHREY BOGART,
JAMES CAGNEY, SIDNEY
GREENSTREET, HUMPHREY
BOGART, JAMES CAGNEY,
GEORGE RAFT, JAMES CAGNEY,
JAMES CAGNEY, JAMES CAGNEY,
JAMES CAGNEY AND HUMPHREY
BOGART . . . AND LAUREN
BACALL AND HUMPHREY
BOGART AND JAMES CAGNEY
AND BETTE DAVIS, BETTE DAVIS
AND EDWARD G. ROBINSON,
AND HUMPHREY BOGART.

'Bum stir crazy stool pigeon hoodlum
cheap hood mobster crummy louse rat
dirty
fink dirty rat cheap bum no good bum
just
a bum a rat a louse a deal square the
cops
we may be rats crooks murderers but
we're
Americans come clean squeal sing fill
you
full of holes no don't shoot let him have
it scram up the ante if I wanted a lecture
I would've went to college you're crazy
she's crazy you think I'm crazy cheap
tramp grand the heat's on the heat's off
please don't shoot some kind of cheap
crook my share you'll get your share he
got his share fair and square rubbed out
taken for a ride you trying to take me
for a ride whistle class that dame's got
class he's got class big time no dice
whistle private eye dick feds cops G-men
T-men just put your lips together and
blow heist punk hijack the big house
Sing Sing I'm from the collection agency
I'm here to collect my wife don't move
or
I'll fill you full of lead you want to
spend your life on the run I don't want to
spend my life on the run don't dont'
shoot
you don't have the guts to use take the
rap showdown the laugh's on you
you rat you don't have the guts to
use it don't make me use it don't
shoot I didn't mean nothing get in
get in the car
get in the boat
get up there get behind the wheel
walk run freeze don't shoot I didn't
mean nothing I don't know so help me
God I don't have it I don't know where
he stashed it put your foot down
he's hot
you're hot
it's hot step on the gas slow down
take it easy let him have it don't
shoot gimme a cigarette will you
some guy in a white convertible
light me a cigarette
I didn't mean nothing, Al

I didn't squeal, Lefty
You know me better than that, Joe
What kept you, Lieutenant
so you're Mr Big okay we can do a deal
what kind of a deal is that
you want out
she wants out
we want out
I want out get out
don't think I want out
no chance no dice no deal there's a
break out tonight it's a break
count me out . . .'

Enter SIR FLUTE PARSONS.
He is tall and thin and hinged at his knees and wearing the tweeds he wears for such occasions when brought up from his country home to meet and treat with Americans and earn money. He is a distinguished and very well respected dramatist who once wrote a very good play indeed and with it went through the Golden Gate, once wrote a very bad film indeed which won all the prizes and became brilliant.
He coughs.
He is ignored. The voices go on and he is ignored.
So he coughs again. Still ignored so he leaves.
Exit SIR FLUTE PARSONS.

'. . . Fall guy, top of the world ma
top of the world
I would hate to spoil your pretty face
you rat I would hate to have to use it
don't shoot I would hate anything to
happen to her
such a pretty young woman if anything
happens to her if anything happens to
me don't think I wouldn't use it
don't shoot we can come to some kind
of arrangement we can make a deal
the safe the money the suitcase the
gold the bonds the statue so beautiful
so many people have died to possess
the safe deposit box
the key the gat the gun
it's been a very pleasant party
Mr Marlowe
such a shame to have to leave
I'm sorry to have to take her with me
such a pretty little thing
leave so early without you sorry I can't
stay the feeling is mutual
sucker sap dumb smart get wise come
clean sing you can tell me keep your trap
shut she's too good for you
I'm not good enough for you
he's too good for you
you think you're good enough for her
a hundred grand bucks dollars two grand
swing for you greenbacks I was
framed I didn't do it I was out of
town it's a frame-up he won't squeal
he knows better than to squeal I'm
no squealer how much do you want to
keep your mouth shut you were meant
to think that the hot seat Death Row
fry burn the chair we can have everything
baby three ways four ways you can have
my share I'll give you my share I'll cut
you in don't shoot you won't shoot
I hope you can swim we can try again I'll
go straight over the border I tried to go
straight you promised me you'd go
straight
you can have everything you want honey
clothes money diamonds a big house
what kind of a joint is this you want out
don't shoot it's not loaded what kind of
a man are you I've had it rich I've had
it poor I'll come out come out with your
hands up we can build a new life it isn't
too late he's dead you've killed him
you liar you cheat you no good bum
what kind of woman do you think I am
I don't want your money I want my share
how much for your silence Mr Nelson
I'll reward you handsomely Mr Angelo
you won't find me ungenerous Mr Patsy
liquor hooch pig swill scotch bourbon
martini manhattan on the rocks hijack
switch ride too many highballs lady
I've had it poor I've had it rich
believe me rich is better it's no crime
to be poor Al I'm just a cheap hoodlum
down on his luck it's no life for a
boy as young as he is what kind of a life
is it on the run always on the run I
want a home I don't want to have to hide
I want kids somewhere we can hide out
until the heats off we may be rats
he's a heel what kind of a racket is
this a sweet little racket that was a
cheap trick you pulled we may be
broads tramps dames you can dish it out
but you can't take it anymore I'll go
anywhere just say it Joe I can't let you
get away with it Joe I'm doing this for
momma Joe I'm doing this for you
Harry I'm doing this for Tony

Vince don't think I'm doing this for
you Lefty I'm doing this for poppa
Momma Al I'm doing this for my kid
sister brother who never had a chance
who could've been a musician lawyer
big shot President of the United States
big time made the grade made the big
time you couldn't make the big time
they never gave me a break the cops
never give a guy a break sure I tried
to go straight I had plenty of chances
I took my chances momma was proud of
you Joe you never gave a sucker an
even break you're scared Joe you're
yellow Joe don't shoot Joe some guy
gives you a break how long has this
been going on, Joe
While your old man's in the penitentiary
you been holding hands with the punk
put him there it's not like that, Joe
believe me, Joe
Miss Dolores was entertaining me while
we awaited your coming, Joe
Sit down, Joe
I regret to have to ask you to put your
hands above your head, Joe
Honest Joe, I can explain everything, Al,
Miss Cotolette would like you to freshen
her drink, Joe
Play it, Sam
we may be rats don't shoot, Joe
Come here, Sidney I want to chastise you
Let him have it, Joe
we may be rats I'm your kind of man
that's
why baby what kind of woman do you
take
me for my kind of woman man I'm not
good
enough for you baby I'm just a cheap
hoodlum down on his luck fink punk bum
Joe oh Joe hold me tight Joe I'm scared
Joe we may be rats we may be crooks we
may be murderers but we're
Americans, Joe'

Or, alternatively JOE VERIATO *has said it all while sitting in one of the chairs.*

2 JOE VERIATO *is a dapper little American with very small feet which are encased in Gucci shoes.
He sits in one of the plastic and ribbon steel chairs, plastic slung chairs which swivel, swing, pitch, roll to any desire and often to their own desire. They are dangerous.*

Enter WESLEY *who is a carbon copy of* JOE VERIATO *or would be if he could be, but he's taller, softer, fatter than* JOE, *less able to control his voice or his movements. He can wear the clothes though and does.
He carries a box of pencils.*

WESLEY: Hi Joe . . .

JOE VERIATO: Yes, that's right I'm Joe. Can I ask you to wait one moment, Wes?

WESLEY: Sure.
Are you listening to something Joe? Are you experiencing something?

JOE VERIATO: I am not prepared, you know what I mean . . . I am going into this thing without preparation.

WESLEY: That is not true.

JOE VERIATO: Thank you, but . . . can we all wait just another moment?

WESLEY: Sure. They're all very talented and sensitive people, they'll understand.

JOE VERIATO *nods shrewdly, comments:*

JOE VERIATO: They're happily hitting the juice, huh?

WESLEY: They're having a few drinks, yes.
Do I place the pencils on the table, Joe?

JOE VERIATO: Sure, you can do that.

WESLEY: You are not going to postpone the meeting?

JOE VERIATO: I am not.

WESLEY: Fine.

JOE VERIATO: What are we here for, Wes?

WESLEY: Sure . . . I can understand doubts.

JOE VERIATO: Well, come on . . .

WESLEY: I'm a slow man, Joe. If you want an answer to a question like that, you got to give me time.

JOE VERIATO: You misunderstand me.

WESLEY: You mean why are we here today?

JOE VERIATO: I mean that.

WESLEY: You mean, facts?

JOE VERIATO: Be my file, Wes . . . don't get smart, just be my file.

WESLEY: You mean why are you here today?

JOE VERIATO: I mean that, yes.

WESLEY: Because I am here today because you are here today, Joe, I am your colleague.

JOE VERIATO: I know that, I hired you.

WESLEY: No, Joe.
The Film Institute of the United States hired me.

JOE VERIATO: Do we have a status anxiety here, Wes? You are my accredited deputy on this project, Wes . . .

WESLEY: I am your assistant, Joe, but I am not here to kiss ass . . .

JOE VERIATO: Whose ass is this we kiss, Wes?

WESLEY: Your ass.

JOE VERIATO: When did we ever kiss my ass, Wes?

WESLEY: Joe . . . Joe . . .

JOE VERIATO: No, come on Wes . . . whose ass are we kissing round here, because we are not kissing my ass, have I ever asked you to kiss ass?

WESLEY: I would rather not pursue the argument.

JOE VERIATO: Right.

WESLEY: You asked me to kiss ass last night in the presence of the Prime Minister and several British senators . . .

JOE VERIATO: That is simply not true.

WESLEY: Okay . . .

JOE VERIATO: Wesley, I want you to contribute.

WESLEY: I contributed . . . I said, why don't we use Americans, it's about Americans, it's our goddam war for Christ sake . . .

JOE VERIATO: That Wesley is the last time I want to hear you or anybody else say that . . .

WESLEY: Why do we need the bastards?

JOE VERIATO: We need their talent.

WESLEY: I don't think so.

JOE VERIATO: I know we disagree on this, Wes . . . but last night was not the time for you to say so . . .

WESLEY: I didn't want to start the whole argument over . . . but . . .

JOE VERIATO: But you did, you did.

WESLEY: I did. I feel strongly about this, very strongly . . . we are talking about America, Joe, it's called we are talking about America, Joe . . . about the birth of America as a nation . . . why can't we use Americans?

JOE VERIATO: We can use Americans. Sure, we can use Americans . . . can you listen to an American speaking Shakespeare?

WESLEY: We are not talking about Shakespeare.

WESLEY: That's what I mean, I just kiss ass around here.

JOE VERIATO: We are talking about a Shakespeare type, *Man for All Seasons* type cast. We need actors with the weight to carry this concept, we got some, they got more . . . we tried Wesley, in the States we asked film-makers to join with us in conceptioning what we require of a movie on the events and ideas of the American Revolution . . . what did they say, they said shit we have not wish to be involved, shit they said . . . right?

WESLEY: They didn't all say shit.

JOE VERIATO: Ninety-nine per cent of those approached said just that . . . what are you talking about, I was the guy assigned the task . . . I was the guy asked these guys, could you just, ah, talk to us, sir?

WESLEY: John Huston didn't say shit, Joe.

JOE VERIATO: No . . . no he didn't.

WESLEY: To his eternal credit, Joe.

JOE VERIATO: Sure.

WESLEY: Right.

JOE VERIATO: So-o why are we here, Wesley?

WESLEY: Why is the Film Institute of the United States here, or why are you here?

JOE VERIATO: Why am I here?

WESLEY: I have to insert a micro-electrode into your brain or something crazy like that to find the answer to that one . . .

JOE VERIATO: Am I so opaque?

WESLEY: No . . .

JOE VERIATO: Right, you know why I'm here.

WESLEY: Okay, you're here because Mel couldn't make it.

JOE VERIATO: I'm here because Mel wouldn't make it . . . because although Mel is assigned as acting chairman of this group he said shit too. Why did Mel say shit, Wes?
I'll tell you and I don't need to enter his very fine cerebellum to know why . . .

WESLEY: He's tied up in Utah.

JOE VERIATO: Right.

WESLEY: The Utes got him.

JOE VERIATO: Right.

WESLEY: The Utes got him tied up in Utah.

JOE VERIATO: Mel has found it very convenient to be tied up in Utah, Wesley, very convenient, you understand?
Now Mel is a first class person, a fine administrator, a fine teaching person. Mel can educate . . . Mel is a fine human being in many ways, but Mel is not the person to conceptualise a major motion picture of exoteric quality which thus far we are deeply comitted to visualise here . . . so he gets tied up in Utah. I love that man, but you know when I heard that he SHRUNK!
He shrunk to be this size!
This size!
Look at me, Wesley, this size . . .

With finger and thumb and screwed up eyes JOE VERIATO *shows how small Mel is become.*

Which is why I am here, and why you are here . . . why we are here . . . don't I get a pencil?

WESLEY: Sure . . .

JOE VERIATO: A carafe of water?

WESLEY: Sure.

Exit WESLEY *leaving* JOE VERIATO *to meditate.*
Re-enter WESLEY *with carafe of water which he places at the right hand of* JOE VERIATO.
Exit JOE VERIATO *from sight, by the swivelling of his chair.*
Exit WESLEY.
Enter SIR FLUTE PARSONS. *The hidden* JOE VERIATO *utters, softly:*

JOE VERIATO: I would like to welcome you all here on behalf of Mel Yarrowbird Jr, who is acting chairman of this group but is unfortunately tied up in Utah with a feature film the Film Institute of the United States is doing on the dispossessing of the American Indian . . .

Enter WESLEY.
Enter with him, SY HOELMERSBAGGER *who is a historian from Yale, with him* CARLF DORF *who is an expatriate film-maker from New York, with them* DANIEL RASHUR *who is tall, diffident, youngish from anywhere, with him* MICKEY BOORMAN *and* PAT SLIGO *from the West Coast, they are very young, very rude, very loutish, very nasty.*
DANIEL RASHUR *is the most pleasant and composed person present. When he disagrees he does so with a quizzical grin, when he agrees he grins wider but looks sceptical. He is gentle and liked.*

WESLEY: It's our first feature film, and . . .

He shrugs, apologises.
MICKEY BOORMAN *and* PAT SLIGO *hug each other and hate each other. They sit together because they don't trust each other.*
Re-enter JOE VERIATO *to back up* WESLEY's *statement of apology with his own brusque:*

JOE VERIATO: Well, I guess we don't need to spell out what that means . . .

WESLEY: Our very first, and . . .

Awkardness. All stand.

JOE VERIATO: I have a little statement here to introduce . . .

WESLEY: Why don't we all sit down?

JOE VERIATO: I would prefer to read the statement because it does condense the whole problem into a few pages, and then we can get on with . . . on to the business of this . . . with some knowledge of what we're supposed to do.

SIR FLUTE: I wonder if I've come to the right place?

WESLEY: You have, Sir Flute.

SIR FLUTE: Thank you. I came in earlier and I coughed . . .

WESLEY: You did? Why was that?

SIR FLUTE: I wished to attract attention.

JOE VERIATO: You wanted to say you were here.

SIR FLUTE: There didn't seem to be anybody here.

WESLEY: I want you to know that we weren't hiding.

JOE VERIATO: And that we're very glad to have you here.

SIR FLUTE: I don't know whether I can help . . .

JOE VERIATO: You can help . . . you and your colleagues . . .

SIR FLUTE: Ah yes . . .
It was arranged that I should have real money.

WESLEY: Of course we won't talk about that now though.

SIR FLUTE: That's up to you, but I hope it is understood that I get real money.

JOE VERIATO: I don't think we deal in counterfeit money . . . Sir Flute . . . I think we deal in dollars.

SIR FLUTE: I'm not sure that I want dollars.

WESLEY: We only have dollars . . . but, some other time, surely, Sir Flute?

SIR FLUTE: Everybody thinks I'm gaga. But I'm not. Half down and half when I leave.

JOE VERIATO: Pardon me?

SIR FLUTE: When you get to my age you don't care about being rude.

JOE VERIATO: I don't care about being rude and I'm a third of your age . . .

SIR FLUTE: Now, that is a lie . . .

WESLEY: Well . . .

SIR FLUTE: Because I am only fifty-three.

JOE VERIATO: You are?

WESLEY: Sure . . .

JOE VERIATO: What's a third of fifty-three?

SIR FLUTE: You're not.

JOE VERIATO: You are so triumphant!

SIR FLUTE: Aren't I?

JOE VERIATO: There are other people here just as distinguished as you are, Sir Flute, who are waiting to contribute . . .

SIR FLUTE: Perhaps they've been paid.

JOE VERIATO: I don't know about that, I guess you're a card . . .

SIR FLUTE: No no, I'm very serious. When you get to my age you want your money now, after all the curtains may be . . .

JOE VERIATO: At fifty-three?

SIR FLUTE: If one is burning the candle at both ends . . .

JOE VERIATO: And you are doing that?

SIR FLUTE: I am trying to.

JOE VERIATO: Why?

SIR FLUTE: Because I'm bored.

JOE VERIATO: Oh my goodness, let's see what we can do about that, Sir Flute, let's see if we can deliver you from boredom . . .

SIR FLUTE: Just as soon as you've paid me.

JOE VERIATO: What am I paying you for?

WESLEY: I think that what Sir Flute is saying . . .

JOE VERIATO: Yes, would you let me handle this . . . ?

WESLEY: Sure.

SIR FLUTE: There isn't anything to be handled.

JOE VERIATO: Do you have an agent?

SY HOELMERSBAGGER: I have flown half way round the world to be present at this?

JOE VERIATO: Sy, my dear friend . . . I am so embarrassed . . . that you should have to listen to this . . . gentlemen . . .

WESLEY: Mr Hoelmersbagger has been travelling for three days to be here, Sir Flute, I think I told you that he is an authority on . . .

SIR FLUTE: Travel?

SY HOELMERSBAGGER: Well, yes, I guess I am.

SIR FLUTE: Were you paid?

SY HOELMBERSBAGGER: I don't think I care to answer that.

CARL DORF: Are you pleading the fifth amendment, Sy?

JOE VERIATO: I don't know what to say to you, Sir Flute, we want you here . . .
I don't know what to say.

SIR FLUTE: Well, you may say what you like and of course I'll stay and listen because I've got nothing better to do and I have come up from the country to be here today and I don't want to be thrown out on the streets because I shall only start drinking if I'm let loose in London . . . other things, do the other things and maybe not get home for years . . . but I shan't contribute, I make it a rule to attend these gatherings, gleanings, only on payment of a fee, do you mind? Is it awfully rude of me? Nevertheless we are a beaten race. We must all do what we can to earn money, our poor country. But do you mind if sitting quiet, quiet quiet, as a mouse, I say nothing until I'm paid?

JOE VERIATO: Wes . . . ?
Will you excuse me for a moment, gentlemen?
Wesley?

JOE VERIATO *tugs* WESLEY *downstage out of earshot, he hopes, to say:*

What the blue fuck has gone wrong here?

WESLEY: I don't know.

JOE VERIATO: Does this character know what we are here for?

WESLEY: Sure.

JOE VERIATO: What's this about money?

WESLEY: I don't know.

JOE VERIATO: Does he know that this project is in no way commercial?

WESLEY: Joe, I don't know. I was asked to gather together certain eminent persons, right? I asked the Film Institute of the United Kingdom, they came up with him and they came up with Carl . . .

JOE VERIATO: Is this their way of saying shit?

WESLEY: I don't think so, he's a very well respected person, an actor, director, writer . . .

JOE VERIATO: Okay, find out what he wants and pay him.

WESLEY: I don't know how to do that.

JOE VERIATO: Don't we have some kind of record of the kind of money these Limey fruits ask for?

WESLEY: I don't think it's quite like that, no . . . no, I don't . . .

JOE VERIATO: Well, I guess you've got to go over there and ask him. Christ, I asked to talk to really eminent people here . . . what do I get?

WESLEY: We don't have to pay him.

JOE VERIATO: No.

WESLEY: We can ask him to leave.

JOE VERIATO: He's the only Limey we've got, Wes . . . he must be some kind of authority, huh?

WESLEY: I believe he is a relative of

General Burgoyne . . .

JOE VERIATO: You mean military co-operation? We can't risk losing the Irish Army . . .

WESLEY: No . . . I mean Saratoga.

JOE VERIATO: We don't have to lose Saratoga.

WESLEY: Somebody did.

JOE VERIATO: Right. Gentleman Johnny, right?
Is he going to feel any kind of resentment? Because I don't want that, I want us to be in concordance.

WESLEY: I don't know.

JOE VERIATO: Do you want to find out for me?

WESLEY: I'm sorry . . .

JOE VERIATO: Right . . . Wes, I love you, but do your fucking job, right?

WESLEY: I guess so . . .

JOE VERIATO: Thank you. Now, as to this situation we have here, can we talk about tactics . . . ?

WESLEY: I don't think we ought to talk at all . . . I think they're beginning to feel that they might as well go home.

JOE VERIATO: Sure, I understand that.

Going back to the others and with a big smile, embracing them all with his arms out gesture:

Gentlemen . . . shall we just sit down and get into it?

SIR FLUTE: As long as you realise that I can't actually say anything.

JOE VERIATO: Okay . . . but, I tell you what I defy you . . . now how about that, I Joe Veriato, defy you . . . how about that? I defy you to remain silent . . . you can't do it, Sir Flute . . .

SIR FLUTE: Oh, I can.

JOE VERIATO: Not here you can't.
Okay . . . you remain silent . . .
gentlemen, I would like to welcome you all . . . you heard all that, let me just say that what we are about to do . . . that what we expect to do . . . that we are going to . . Wes, do you want to sit down?

WESLEY: I don't know . . . here we are, but have we got off on a bad start here?
I mean, there is a person here feels some kind of resentment . . . I think I got to go and talk to his agent . . . you know what I mean.

A roar of laughter from all those present. SIR FLUTE *doesn't join in.*

JOE VERIATO: They know what you mean.

PAT SLIGO: I don't know what you mean, I don't talk to agents . . . such like creeps.

MICKEY DOORMAN: Right.

PAT SLIGO: We're not into that.

JOE VERIATO: Pat, we know that.
Pat, Mickey, Sy, Carl . . . did we meet somewhere before, New York?

WESLEY: Carl can't go to New York, Joe.

JOE VERIATO: Is that so? Well, you are not missing too much believe me . . .
Dan.
Why can't he go to New York? (*An aside to* WESLEY *as they all sit down.* WESLEY *about to exit.*)

WESLEY: It's quite a famous case, Joe.

Exit WESLEY.

JOE VERIATO: Come back here, Wes . . .

Re-enter WESLEY.

You want to get cute? Be my guest.

WESLEY: I want to arrange something for Sir Flute . . .

JOE VERIATO: Allow me to handle this, Wes, I want you here.

WESLEY: Can't I just ask my secretary to see what she can do, she can hack this . . .

JOE VERIATO: I want you back here.

WESLEY: Sure, but let me just . . .

JOE VERIATO: I can't go into this without you here, Wes . . . I don't want you pedaddling around while I'm putting our case here . . .

WESLEY: Right.
Why don't we just ask him?

JOE VERIATO: Right . . . Sir Flute, could you step into the office just a moment, I'm sorry gentlemen, but we seem to have a problem here.
Sir Flute?

SIR FLUTE *gets up from the table and comes down to join them.*

WESLEY: We would like to know just what kind of money we are talking about, Sir Flute?

JOE VERIATO: Just an idea, then we can approach your agent . . .

SIR FLUTE: No no, I want real money, in my hand . . . now . . . I was asked to come this morning, but I couldn't get here until this afternoon, I must leave this evening whatever happens, but I shall want paying for the whole day, so perhaps you would rather do without me?

JOE VERIATO: How much?

SIR FLUTE: Fifty pounds?

JOE VERIATO: Sure.

SIR FLUTE: Twenty-five pounds now and twenty-five when I leave.

WESLEY: We can manage that.
I'll go and arrange that . . .

JOE VERIATO *takes out his wallet, looks through it, credit cards, a ten pound note.*

JOE VERIATO: Do you have any money, Wes?

WESLEY *looks in his wallet, finds a five pound note, some loose change. Shows it.*

Ask the boys . . .

WESLEY: I can go out and get it.

JOE VERIATO: No. We have wasted the morning already.

WESLEY: Now that was not my fault, Joe, you were not prepared.

JOE VERIATO: Do you want me to go into this project, a project like this, unprepared?
I want this settled here and now, ask Sy, Dan . . . look fellas, forgive me but, do you have any money?

SY HOELMBERSBAGGER: How much do you need, Joe?

CARL DORF: No.

WESLEY: Can you give me thirty-five pounds, Sy?

SY HOELMBERSBAGGER: I don't think I have that . . . just let me see if I have that, I have Turkish lira, I guess I should've done something about that . . . I've been on a dig . . .

MICKEY BOORMAN: I got it.

JOE VERIATO: We don't need that much, we only need ten . . .

All the Americans gathered together round the table, opening their wallets, looking for money, thrusting money at WESLEY.

WESLEY: No, Joe, no . . . we need ten and then we need the second payment of twenty-five if you are not going to let me go out and rob the bank or something . . . is that not right, Sir Flute?
You want twenty-five now and twenty-five when you leave, right?

SIR FLUTE, *standing aloof from all this, nods.*

SIR FLUTE: Absolutely.

JOE VERIATO: I see.

WESLEY: Thank you, Sir Flute.

MICKEY BOORMAN: I got it, how much do you need? I got it here . . . huh?

WESLEY: Thank you, Mickey. We can see the kind of films you make . . .

MICKEY BOORMAN *thrusts a bundle of notes at* WESLEY, *shrugs, grins.*

Thank you.

JOE VERIATO: Now that we have settled this somewhat embarrassing . . .

SIR FLUTE: I'm not the least bit embarrassed you know, not the least.

JOE VERIATO: Okay . . .

CARL DORF: Why did it take you three days to get here, Sylvane?

SY HOELMERSBAGGER: No reason, I guess I took my time.

JOE VERIATO: Well, we're sure glad you got here.

WESLEY: Sy is an authority on the history of America, but you all know that, I guess.

JOE VERIATO: Okay . . . we want to produce a feature film based on the highest quality of scholarly content and cinematic achievement . . .

WESLEY: I think they know that, Joe.

JOE VERIATO: Okay, Wes, so they know that.

WESLEY: I think they all received an agenda in the mail which said that . . . I hope so.

JOE VERIATO: I'd like to open the discussion, Wes.

WESLEY: Joe, may I just say something first?

JOE VERIATO: Well yes, but I wanted to say to open the discussion that Wesley has some ideas how we should open the discussion, because we want you to say things here, but we don't want to range over the entire spectrum here, we want to get down to specifics if we can, I know I speak for Mel when I say this . . . let's try to be constructive and specific, I mean I have worked for major motion picture studios in the past and I know that wide ranging over the whole entire spectrum is counter-productive, let's think before we speak and let's kind of put into this . . . and I can be as tough as a bootheel you know, I want results, I don't want anything we can't use, I want structure, and I know Mel would want the same . . . only Mel is tied up in Utah and can't tell you himself . . . but Wesley can tell you for him, go ahead now, Wesley . . . oh but first let me tell you that there have been a lot of sore comments about why are we doing this in England . . . well, why are we doing this film about the birth of our nation in England? Let me tell you why . . .

WESLEY: Can I say something here, Joe.

JOE VERIATO: Well, yes but I was about to say . . .

WESLEY: I don't want everybody to feel they . . . well, they might get the wrong idea about what Mel wants here . . . in terms of the way we structure this thing, Mel wants there to be the widest possible ranging over the spectrum, he hopes we can leave it as unstructured as possible and sort of what . . . we're basically trying to range as wide as we can . . . I think we're best off to leave the thing as unstructured as possible . . . just sort of develop a laundry list out of it, keep it as open as possible all down the line . . . I mean I want to say, don't be locked into thinking about this as the standard two-hour documentary for television or a feature . . . we can approach it a number of different ways and you know we can come up with some very crazy ideas . . .
Joe?

SIR FLUTE: George Washington had dreadful teeth you know . . .

A silence.
Then SY HOELMERSBAGGER *asks cuttingly:*

SY HOELMBERSBAGGER: Is that your first five pounds worth?

CARL DORF: I think I knew that.

JOE VERIATO: Is that so, Sir Flute? Now that is very interesting, that is so . . . that is as interesting as Napoleon and his haemorrhoids . . . those are the sort of crazy things we want to throw around here . . . Dan?

JOE VERIATO *concentrates on* DANIEL RASHUR *for a moment. This happens quite often. Because* DANIEL RASHUR *rarely says anything, he is treated with immense respect by everyone and always included in the conversation. There are times when those present seem to feel that he has enormous importance, he becomes the pivot of the entire meeting. He now smiles at* JOE VERIATO *amiably and listens.*

You know Dan, we're looking for a flame, do you know what I mean, Dan? Dan, we don't know what kind of a flame it will be . . . but?

CARL DORF: Is this thing open?

JOE VERIATO: Well.
Let me think how I can answer that, Carl, Dan . . . I imagine you are

surprised that we haven't found somebody within the Institute, some young film maker . . . I too, I too . . . you might have taken it for granted that Fellows associated with, or oblique have made films for the Institute before, and have done well by oblique for the . . . er . . . would be the people we might consider, you know, certainly foremost, Dan . . . but no, Carl, no Dan, what is going to happen is that this flame thing is going to be ignited by anyone, anyone at all, it can be anyone, a guy off the street can come into this room, it can be anyone . . . sure, he can be a Fellow of the Institute or just anybody in the film making community, and now we have gone into partnership with the Film Institute of the United Kingdom we have to include their community, and they might indeed come forward with a response to what we generate, faithfully reported by you, Carl . . . Sir Flute . . . come forth eager to explore this with us, anyone . . .

CARL DORF: What you are trying to say is that this thing is open to anybody . . .

WESLEY: Exactly.

PAT SLIGO: Blah blah blah . . .

JOE VERIATO: Thank you Pat . . . is that going to be your contribution?

PAT SLIGO *and* MICKEY BOORMAN *have treated all this with sniggering contempt, have hugged and nudged each other with delight whenever the mood has taken them, have passed each other scribbled notes, made great play of being bored, irritated.*

PAT SLIGO: I'll have more to say if it gets more relevant . . . I mean I'm here to talk about a Revolution, right? I know that Mickey feels the same way. Right?

MICKEY BOORMAN: Sure, but you know how I like to think, I like to think in terms of something we don't have here, I want to forget that we're into any hide-bound image of early American history you know funny hats and lean men with long rifles chewing bits of goddam buffalo, you know . . . can I say I'm not entirely sure that I should be here, I don't want to be rude, but I can see why Pat might be here, sure, but me? Come on now . . . huh?

PAT SLIGO: That's really something, you know, that's brotherly . . . woweeee, you Benedict Arnold you, that's really off the wall . . .

MICKEY BOORMAN: I don't see what's so off the wall about it?

PAT SLIGO: If you don't see why you should be here why the hell should I be here, what's so special about your approach Mickey . . . huh? I respect you and I love you but screw you . . . huh? Screw you!

MICKEY BOORMAN: Come on . . . you dig this kind of shit, music, dramatic, plot films . . . one screen sitting there finger fucking, Julie Christie coming out at you saying which way to the goddam revolution George, you know . . .

PAT SLIGO: I don't think I said that.

MICKEY BOORMAN: I don't think I said that.

MICKY BOORMAN: You know funny hats and lean men with long rifles you know . . .

JOE VERIATO: Well . . .

MICKEY BOORMAN: Well, I would need one hundred hours of film . . . I mean Pat likes to think he's . . . well, but he's joy-riding that's all, he puts together some heavy words you know Buckminster Fuller and Joyce and you know music . . . I would need money and I would need one hundred hours of film and I would need no interference . . . no interdictions from you or anybody, ten years it's gonna take ten years but I can do some kind of nostalgic type trip . . . you know drama is obsolete, you know, art has no reason to play with drama any more you know, really not . . .

JOE VERIATO: Hey . . . I don't think . . . ten years, I don't think we can wait ten years . . . I mean next year is optimum . . . well '76 is the year, I guess we can take in '77/'78/'79 but . . . eighty six?
I don't know . . . our brief is '76, it's an emotive time and well . . .

MICKEY BOORMAN: Next year!

JOE VERIATO: Right, well we don't

have to show it next year, like I said seventy-seven, seventy-eight but . . . eighty-six is not possible . . .

PAT SLIGO: I can give you something next year . . .

WESLEY: Can I come in here?

JOE VERIATO: I'd be pleased to have you do so, Wes . . . hey, you know we're talking, huh?

JOE VERIATO *is very pleased, he beams, rubs his hands, chuckles.*

We got a dialogue going here.

SY HOELMBERSBAGGER: I have said very little yet . . .

JOE VERIATO: There's time, Sy there's time.

WESLEY: Can I come in here?

SY HOELMBERSBAGGER: What I would like to interject here . . .

WESLEY: I don't think we want to ask those of us who are here today . . .

SY HOELMERSBAGGER: I think I'm going to say the same thing that you are going to say, Wesley . . .

WESLEY: Well, why can't I say it?

JOE VERIATO (*soothingly*): You can say it, Wesley . . . now hush yo' mouth while Sy is saying it . . .

SY HOELMERSBAGGER: I don't want to
step on any corns here . . . but are we going to go to all the established writers and directors and say to them, this you can take and do in your own way, you know . . people as eminent as John Ford, John Bean, John Huston . . . I have immense respect, I have reverence for them and hopefully they will be wanting to do something here. But, are we going to ask such people to do something which comes out of what we are hopefully going to say today, the result of this group's inspiration if you like, which I think would be insulting to suchlike people I have just mentioned, I mean they are . . . they are the image makers, I can't see them needing what we have to say, glory be, or . . . or are we going to go to clean in that sense, I'm not going to say anything else . . . I guess I mean pure, in that they haven't actually perhaps done anything in cinematic terms, I guess I mean virginal so far as the body of work they might have to offer . . . I guess I mean they haven't done anything but they are so full of desire to create movies . . . or are we going to them to say
humbly, say to them this is the most awful, and I mean that to be spelt with an actual 'e', the most full of awe thing we . . . and the most frightfully complex thing to drop into your lap young man, young film maker, but be not dismayed, tell us what our American Revolution means to you, some fresh young monkey with dreams . . . and you are going to have trouble doing it, but we are here to help you . . .

PAT SLIGO: We are behind you . . .

MICKEY BOORMAN: Heh!

SY HOELMERSBAGGER: Wholly . . .

MICKEY BOORMAN: Heh!

SY HOELMERSBAGGER: . . . whole heartedly,
and do it next year, or for next year, or for next year, young man, it being the Bicentennial upcoming . . . I don't see why he can't be making the movie during the whole of the period you have just mentioned, Joe, just mentioned, this being our festival, Dan, our celebration if you like, Dan . . . work through . . . I doubt if Mickey can have his ten years, his ten years, but . . . ?

JOE VERIATO: Ten months, Mickey? Wes?

WESLEY: I just wanted to say that.

JOE VERIATO: You know, you have said something there, Sy, which we should think about . . .

SY HOELMBERSBAGGER: Think about it . . .

WESLEY: And I also want to say that John Bean is hoping to be with us later, so . . .

CARL DORF: I want to question the whole question of is this going to be just one movie, Joe, Dan, Pat, Wes . . . are we not being too . . . too . . . ?

WESLEY: I would say, blinkered.

CARL DORF: That's right.

SY HOELMERSBAGGER: How many motion pictures are we talking about?

CARL DORF: That's my question.

JOHN VERIATO: Alright sure . . . all right. But Sy, baby, Sy . . . to get to discussing your point of view which, which has distance, I mean it stretches, it takes in the prairies, you know what I mean?
Sure, what you say about the patronisation we should be doing of the younger forces in the visual arts oblique cinema today, which we are all part of . . . yes, I say yes there is no doubt about it, rather than the older more established type artist, there is no question about it . . . but, but Sir Flute who is still here . . . even he, young in heart . . .

SIR FLUTE: I'm not at all young in any way . . . no no . . .

JOE VERIATO: Sure baby, sure you are, look at your whole . . . your . . . look at your necktie!
Only someone with a sense of humour could . . . only a person . . . gay and laughterful . . . only . . . but I don't know how I got on to this, we don't want to waste time on personalities . . . what we were saying, the young forces in the cinema, they . . . their youth, that's why the Institute exists, Sy!
Why we're all here today . . . there is no reason why we should go to the Warner Bros. type, I mean baby, huh . . . come on, that way you really would have long men with mean rifles . . . I mean everything so goddam buffalo, we've got to give new forces the chance to go into this thing, and the whole spirit of the thing has to be new and has to be coming from the people for whom the thing is primarily meant and I think that is the young forces and young audiences of today, I think they got to be into this thing we have here from the beginning . . . I mean the way I see it, sure we're having a good time here, over here, in this wonderful country, England but there are redcoats here baby, there really are, they are very charming and very pleased to have us here . . . they're even putting up most of the front money . . . but it *was a revolution,* huh? England is British, we got to remember that . . . and we have our own redcoats here today, and very charming he is, a very charming person, but we got to remember what it was all about, it was about oppression . . . they were not charming you know, they taxed very heavily and all that, they said you got to do this or else, you got to do that, you got to have a King . . . you got to pay for . . .

SIR FLUTE: And why not?

JOE VERIATO: Right!
Right. I want that! I want that point of view, I really do, I want someone to stand up and say shit . . .

SIR FLUTE: I wouldn't dream of . . .

WESLEY: Now why do you want that to happen, Joe . . . ? I think we can get on better than that, people shouting their mouth off about . . . I don't think we need that . . .

CARL DORF: I want to say that I'm not sure we had a revolution.

JOE VERIATO: We had a revolution.

MICKEY BOORMAN: In my opinion we still ain't had no revolution . . .

PAT SLIGO: Now why do you talk like that, Stepin Fetchit?

WESLEY: It's a point of view. Dan?

SY HOELMERSBAGGER: It has some validity.

JOE VERIATO: Oh no, oh no baby, if we're going to do this thing it has got to be a real Revolution or it doesn't go . . . I tell you that. I don't want to know, and the Film Institute of the U.S. does not want to know about an American Revolution film that is not revolutionary, I could not go out and peddle that to anyone . . .

CARL DORF: I don't find any discipline in this. Why?

SY HOELMERSBAGGER: We're trying to broaden the assignment, Dan, within the orbit of the Revolution, which might mean that young people could, say

. . . do a film about now even, or any time in the last couple of hundred years which said what the whole thing was about . . .

CARL DORF: About? What was it about?

SY HOELMERSBAGGER: Hopefully they'll tell us what it was about, it was about.

MICKEY BOORMAN: You mean we can do what we like, like what we like, just so long as we call it . . .

SY HOELMERSBAGGER: Sure, I don't see why not . . . why not.

WESLEY: Why not indeed.

JOE VERIATO: No! No there is a general expectation that this film be set in the historical period which has come to be known as the period of the American Revolution . . .

MICKEY BOORMAN: You mean goddam thee's and thou's and three-ways looking hats and Valley Forge and our Germans against their Germans and why do I have to go to war Pop, because we want to be free son, looking like Henry goddam Fonda?

JOE VERIATO: Yes . . .

WESLEY: He doesn't mean that . . .

PAT SLIGO: If you ask me as a film-maker and you asked me to try to look at this thing . . .

WESLEY: We actually ought to say . . .

PAT SLIGO: I don't know anything about
this time, I don't know anything about the Revolution, if somebody tells me, starts pointing out to me the seeds of what started what, like the seeds of what started what . . . what were the conditions at the time . . . let's thing about the Boston Tea Party, there are a lot of things
I just found out about the Boston Tea Party, just because I knew I was coming here today . . . that I never knew. I always
believed it was what I learned in the first grade, you know sort of life the myths you put away in the back of your mind . . . but I was talking to this guy who is a professor of history in one of the schools around here, one of the colleges
around here and he told me things I suddenly
got into . . . and he was just telling me about it, you know and I started sending it . . . I started working on the film. I can see a film coming here, a film that would be exciting, dramatic and yet absolutely nothing going beyond the fact if you see what I mean . . . if you understand
what I mean . . .

WESLEY: I feel we ought to say here and
now that we didn't have any one person in mind to make this film and that we certainly wouldn't assign any person here today to make this film, that should have been said right at the start here, I tried to say it . . . but, things go racing ahead don't they? . . . don't they? and . . . I don't want to thwart any inspiration, rather I want to stimulate discussion, but anyway I would imagine you are all too busy with your already overfull work program to take on this assignment. We don't have it in mind to ask anyone here . . . we really don't. Mel wanted us to make that clear from the outset.

There is a silence.
SY HOELMERSBAGGER *breaks the silence.*

SY HOELMERSBAGGER: I would not presume, I would not think that I . . . I have nothing to offer except . . . I just wouldn't know how to make a movie, I'm just here to help in putting some ideas together, in an historical context, an historical . . .

MICKEY BOORMAN: Not me, baby, I could not stay in there . . . not this . . .

CARL DORF: What . . . is this subsequent film . . . hopefully . . . is it to be shown commercially?

PAT SLIGO: I can do it.

JOE VERIATO: That's the spark I want. I don't see any reason why the regular film makers in this group should be . . . I don't think Mel had that in mind . . .

PAT SLIGO: I don't know that I

want . . .

WESLEY: No. I have to come in here. I have to tell you that Mel stated quite clearly he didn't want anyone of this group to be asked to . . . well, it is possible that he didn't think we were . . . right?

CARL DORF: Would you like to explain to me why we're here?

JOE VERIATO: You know why you're here, Carl . . .

CARL DORF: We're not going to be given the privilege to put in our bids for this assignment?

WESLEY: No, no I guess not.

JOE VERIATO: I don't think Mel would want any flame that may be ignited to be quenched . . . I don't think I've noticed any real flame yet . . . Dan?

CARL DORF: I can't work in America, do you know that? I was forced to leave the country of my birth. I left a lot of friends who looked the other way if I met them in the street, Dan . . . I didn't mind that, such friends! Such friends are they worth having? But, I left my work, Dan . . . is that what the Revolution was about? I was smeared, I was black-listed, I was unable to work in my chosen profession of screenwriter, so I came to England where I have been allowed to work . . so, you know, what does that say about our Revolution, Dan, Sy, Pat?

MICKEY BOORMAN: I can answer that . . .

JOE VERIATO: I don't think we had such as McCarthy in mind, I don't think so, no, rather we have Thomas Jefferson in mind, Sam Adams in mind, Gunning Bedford Jr, stuff like that.
I have the greatest respect for you, Carl, but I don't know why you're here if you are set on turning this thing into some kind of political angle, these were the men in our country at this time, great men, they really were . . . John Dickinson, stuff like that . . .

SY HOELMERSBAGGER: I for one am astonished that we have taken such a long time to get around to talking properly about George Washington . . .

SIR FLUTE: I did mention . . .

SY HOELMERSBAGGER: You know there was a time when we would have been talking only about George Washington . . .

JOHN BEAN: John Wayne has always wanted to play Washington.

3 He has entered unobtrusively. He is a very old and very shaggy man with a commanding presence. He stands stooping, blinking, peering at the little group of people.
JOHN BEAN *continues.*

JOHN BEAN: You got to think in terms of production and audiences here. John Wayne. Have John Wayne to play Washington.
It's his biggest ambition in life to play George Washington.

JOE VERIATO: Well, Mr Bean, I guess I don't have to tell everyone who you are?

JOHN BEAN: Nope, I guess not.

WESLEY: Glad you could get here, Mr Bean . . .

JOHN BEAN: Do I know you, son?

WESLEY: Wesley . . .

JOHN BEAN: Well, sit down Wes, you look like an intelligent person to me, do you think you could get to like me?

WESLEY: Pardon me?

JOHN BEAN: People are never sure. I know I can get on with you because you've got a frank, open, American face. I could use you, Wes.

WESLEY: I've got a job, Mr Bean.

JOHN BEAN: How long do you think you'll keep your job?

WESLEY: It isn't quite like that . . .

JOHN BEAN: You made one mistake today, I allow one mistake with people who work for me, so-ooooo you got one more mistake should you work for me, only one, most people don't make it, they like to keep it in hand . . . can you cook?

WESLEY: Why am I the subject of this?

JOHN BEAN: I'm looking for somebody who can cook, who can combine the duties of personal assistant and cook, you look as if you can cook.

WESLEY: I really don't think that I am available for such a post . . . I don't want to be a cook.

JOHN BEAN: Don't despise cooking, young man . . . you like eating?
You do.
People made mistakes in the American Revolution you know, a lot of mistakes. Let me tell you all about the mistake young Wesley here made today, he made the mistake of assuming that I knew where to come, and he made the mistake of assuming that I am not a very busy man, he also made the mistake of assuming that I would want to come on the piece of paper I was given.
As a matter of fact one of those mistakes wasn't a mistake at all, because I saw the words 'American Revolution' on that piece of paper and the rest of the bullshit, pardon me Harvard men, the rest of the bullshit didn't matter, but I saw those words and I am here, humbly to offer myself, my skills and my talent the hands of a creator, the mind of man who has seen much,
the heart of an American who is descended from those Americans took up arms against transgressions on their freedom . . . I throw in the fact that my bicentennial forbear was a top sergeant in the British Army but he deserted . . .

JOE VERIATO: Why was that?

JOHN BEAN: My name is Bean, you are?

JOE VERIATO: Joe Veriato . . .

JOHN BEAN: Well, Joe . . . he was Irish.

SIR FLUTE: Two thirds of the British Army was Irish at the time, they didn't desert . . .

JOHN BEAN: I know that voice, I do not
see you because there is sunlight in my eyes, often there is sunlight in my eyes, I am not afraid to reach for the sun, I am not afraid to look foolish because I looked into the sun . . . I am not frightened of confessing that occasionally I am blinded by my ambition . . . am I talking to Flutey?

SIR FLUTE: You are.

JOHN BEAN: We have never met.

SIR FLUTE: We have.

JOHN BEAN: No, believe me . . .

SIR FLUTE: At a party in New York.

JOHN BEAN: No.

SIR FLUTE: Yes.

JOHN BEAN: No, when I say no, I am trying to tell you something Flutey.

SIR FLUTE: I wish I knew what.

JOHN BEAN: Believe me . . .

JOE VERIATO: I think that John is trying to protect you, Sir Flute, I don't know what you got up to at that party but John is endeavouring to give you an out concerning this wild party, hopefully he wishes to save you any embarrassment any revelation regarding the party might have on any . . . body here . . . I guess I'm dying to know what you did, what can you have done?

SIR FLUTE: I was there with Frank.

JOHN BEAN: Flutey, you were not at that party. I want you to believe it.

SIR FLUTE: Only my friends call me Flutey.
Dear friends from childhood, or nice people I have grown to like . . . you have absolutely no right to call me anything other than Flute Parsons, or Sir Flute . . . I don't insist on Sir Flute but I hate being called Mr Parsons, it sounds like I run a shop.
I met you once, Mr Bean . . .

JOHN BEAN: I'm a Chevalier . . . you know.

SIR FLUTE: Really? I didn't know his family awfully well . . . I met you once, Mr Bean, and we said very little because you didn't seem awfully interested in Frank or I, wished to move on, you did, you didn't seem awfully well . . .

JOHN BEAN: Frank whom?

SIR FLUTE: Nobody you would know.

JOHN BEAN: Well, thank you . . . that at least is settled between us . . . I don't have to go into any long and involved denial of any relationship between Frank whomever and myself before these distinguished people here, distinguished movie makers, here assembled . . .

SIR FLUTE: You met him.

JOHN BEAN: Thank you. It should be clear to you by now, Flutey, that I do not wish to pursue this.

SIR FLUTE: As a person he's instantly forgetable . . . poor Frank. Do you remember his second name?

JOHN BEAN: No.

SIR FLUTE: No, neither do I, I was much more interested in meeting you. Still, he was very sweet, Frank . . . he was American, was he a musician?
He smoked pot.
You got beastly drunk and peed in a pot plant, then you fell out of the window when her husband hit you, I didn't know you knew her, apparently you did and had done all the previous week when she was supposed to be in Paris . . .
That was the time when only musicians smoked pot and nobody minded overmuch it seemed, I think that if Frank wasn't a musician he was being awfully brave and go ahead, wasn't he? Awfully.
Without an 'e'.
I say it a lot, it's nervousness. But don't take advantage of it please, it isn't that kind of nervousness.
How nice to meet you again, I thought we were in one of those dreadful skyscraper things. Of course I knew, because we have mutual friends, and I've seen your name. But you know how it is with living legends, one can always imagine them dead.
So, you picked yourself up and carried on where you left off, good for you.
I wish I could.
If I could, I wouldn't be here today.

JOHN BEAN: Do you know, I don't remember any of that, that must have been some party!

SIR FLUTE: It wasn't really, it didn't seem to get going again after you left, very draughty, I caught a cold and Frank got bored.

JOHN BEAN: Carl . . . I can't work with you . . .

SIR FLUTE: It isn't sufficient reason to say that you're Irish, being Irish doesn't explain everything you know . . . And one should never be proud of desertion.

JOHN BEAN: You left your country, Carl.

CARL DORF: I left my country because I was being persecuted, John.

JOHN BEAN: You were a member of the Communist Party in 1937, Carl.

CARL DORF: I never denied that, John.

JOHN BEAN: I cannot work with you.

CARL DORF: I do not wish to work with you.

JOHN BEAN: I believe in freedom, Carl.

CARL DORF: So did I, John.

JOHN BEAN: I believe you would destroy our country, Carl.

CARL DORF: I believe you believe that, John.

JOHN BEAN: I cannot stay in the same room you inhabit.

CARL DORF. I won't put you to any more discomfort, John.

JOHN BEAN: I have never denied your considerable abilities as a film-maker, Carl.

CARL DORF: I have always seen great potential in your work, John.

JOHN BEAN: I feel however that this ability you possess makes you more dangerous.

CARL DORF: I feel you are now however far too old to realise that potential.

JOHN BEAN: I am not much older than you, Carl.

CARL DORF: I am finished as an innovator, John.

JOHN BEAN: I am not finished as anything, Carl.

CARL DORF: I think you are finished as a human being, John.

JOHN BEAN: I think you would like to believe that.

CARL DORF: I think you are a monster, John.

JOHN BEAN: I think you are a has-been, Carl.

CARL DORF: I think I am too, John.

JOHN BEAN: I think that if you know that I can use you, Carl.
Do you want to work with me on this?

CARL DORF: I . . . I don't know what to say.

JOHN BEAN: You used to be a damn good writer, Carl . . .

CARL DORF: I am not any more.

JOHN BEAN: I think you are.

CARL DORF: I don't know how you know that.

JOHN BEAN: I know.

CARL DORF: I am flattered, but . . .

JOHN BEAN: I am serious, Carl.

CARL DORF: I am . . . nonplussed.

JOHN BEAN: I am deeply serious, Carl.

CARL DORF: I am sure you are, John.

JOHN BEAN: I am, believe me.

CARL DORF: I am not sure we can . . .

JOHN BEAN: I am sure.

CARL DORF: I am going to have to think about this . . .

JOHN BEAN: I am not going to give you time, Carl.

CARL DORF: Oh.

JOE VERIATO: I am stunned!

WESLEY: I am not sure that we aren't out of line here.

JOHN BEAN: I am asking Carl to work with me.

JOE VERIATO: I am knocked out . . .

JOHN BEAN: I am asking you all to work with me, humbly . . . I am asking you humbly to turn to this . . .

MICKEY BOORMAN: I am not going to pretend that I have any respect for your movies, Mr Bean . . . I think they're pretty good shit, Mr Bean.

JOHN BEAN: Well they've given a great deal of pleasure to a great many people, perhaps people like shit, Mr Boorman.
As long as it's pretty good shit.
Let me tell you, Mickey, I've seen a lot of your work and I like it. I have the greatest respect for your camera and for your integrity as a film-maker, your pictures make me laugh and they make me horny, and I am an old man and I am very grateful to you . . .

MICKEY BOORMAN *and* PAT SLIGO *roar with laughter at this, hug each other with delight. Then* MICKEY BOORMAN *releases himself from the hysterical clutches of* PAT SLIGO *and says seriously, too seriously to be sincere it seems:*

MICKEY BOORMAN: Let me shake you by the hand, Mr Bean . . .

JOHN BEAN: No, I don't think so, I don't think we need go that far . . .

Let me tell you . . . in the American Revolution there is something for everybody,
let me tell you there was enough violence
tar and feathers,
riding on a rail,
let me tell you there was sex too,
I can't see anybody going without,
this was brought about by real people
with real urges, something not generally considered . . this was a popular revolution.
Have you considered that? You know people
wanted this revolution to happen,
oh yes, this revolution happened from the bottom, thus was it,
yes the generality, and the commonality
from grievous oppression rose up
ordinary cuss and roar
and hammer and saw *People*!
and Harvard men . . . we don't know a damn thing about them,
huh? We know about the rich and the powerful, we know about the lawyers and the merchants, we know about

Washington . . . we know about
Jefferson,
but we don't know a damn thing
to this day about the ordinary guys
who filled the harbour of Boston with tea,
and they liked tea,
ordinary people, some of whom didn't
even have a note . . . so . . . ordinary
people, so there was sex, and you
can show it, should you be so
inclined . . . there was a practice
known as bundling. I don't know that
you Harvard men will be acquainted with
the practice . . . but I had Maureen
O'Hara play a very daring scene in
which she indulged in bundling . . . so,
I can stretch a point,
and they can get caught in the rain,
and they can sport under waterfalls,
and they can take a bath once in a while
our romantic interest, I can take a
bundling scene, I can stretch a point
and you can show me tits,
hell they had tits didn't they? Even
though the Daughters of the Revolution
might not like it, they had tits . . . some
might have had good ample tits,
it can come,
we do not inhabit a barren land here,
this America of ours at this time was a
very abundant place,
stallions prinked,
marcaronis pranced,
there was a fullness of good things you
know, that place we were born flowed,
words, words with edges to them
set, thumped, drenched in ink and
slammed
before thirsty eyes, we can sprawl some
spike some, this movie doesn't have to
be barren, without colour, without balls,
I am come here with a *fever,*
my soul it swells so that I am a *size*
I can accommodate it . . . let me tell you
bundling was men and women sleeping
together so they could get to know each
other, which is considerably liberal so
near to Philadelphia,
but clothes were not removed and a board
was placed between, many is the maiden
remained a maiden for they were not
animals
our progenitors,
no more than may be, people do not
tend to
be animals though oppressed, though
poor,
they tend to remain properly upright
in their condition, they are often
thoughtful doers, they can make a
Revolution, Daniel . . . without the
help of the rich families who ruled
our colony at that time and rode
our backs for some time to come,
tossed up by events,
taken from beneath by popular seas
and reaching for cocked hats to coup
the crise,
withal . . . the lawyers, the planters,
damn sure they didn't know what they
rode, what it was swept them along,
a sweaty swell of *people* it was, sir,
and there was a man,
you know him Harvard men, there was a
man of the *People* . . . you know him,
now . . . now I know a guy who has
always
burned up to portray the role of Tom
Paine, and I can get him, Daniel, I can,
I can . . . you can't get him for ten years
no matter how much you may lie you can
offer . . . but I know should I . . . ? He
will go to his lawyers and he will say
you got to get me out of this fellas,
for I am Tom Paine and I burn to
portray him.
and I don't know how much it may cost
me to obtain my release from this
present motion picture crap I am
contracted to humour but friends I
am going to be Tom Paine for John Bean
and the Film Institute of the United
States in this joint venture we are
entering into . . .

WESLEY: Joe, I don't know that we can
endorse this thinking . . .

JOE VERIATO: I am quietly
exultant . . .

A match is struck by PAT SLIGO.
He waves it, grins evilly and
crows, flicking the lighted match
in an arc over JOE VERIATO:

PAT SLIGO: Hey Joe, we got a spark
here . . . !

MICKEY BOORMAN *yelps with*
delight, grabs for the match box:

MICKEY BOORMAN: That's right . . .
hey Joe, we got a spark.

WESLEY *stamps on the match,*
looks at JOE VERIATO *who seems to*

have gone into a trance, gazing on JOHN BEAN.

WESLEY: Joe . . .

JOE VERIATO: Wesley, I am coolly ecstatic here . . .

WESLEY: I am honestly aghast!

PAT SLIGO *and* MICKEY BOORMAN *strike matches and flick them at* JOE VERIATO.
At JOHN BEAN, *at everyone.*

SY HOELMERSBAGGER: I've been waiting, hoping to say hello,
Mr Bean . . .

JOHN BEAN: We can take care of hellos
later, Harvard man . . . at this moment
I am asking humbly that I be given
this assignment, put it into my hands
gentlemen, I am blue for this,
down here I ache for this,
down here in my crotch, blue . . . I
ache, put it into my hands and work
with me on this, all of you.
All of you.
I ask you humbly . . . no no no no!
Humbly I *demand*!
Give me the American Revolution!
I can *stay*!
Put it into my hands . . . please.

MICKEY BOORMAN: We're with you, John!

WESLEY *steps on another match.*
Exit WESLEY *looking for a fire extinguisher.*

JOHN BEAN: Carl? Dan? Harvard Man?

PAT SLIGO: We're with you, John, you can do it, John . . . I have just begun to fight, baby . . . because we gotta be free . . .

JOHN BEAN: Right, right . . .
and you can script it, Carl, ordinary people right?
And you can do the English, Flutey, right?
Let me tell you how I see it, let me tell you how we open . . .

Matches being struck and flicked over JOHN BEAN *as he sits down in his chair and leans forward to expand, elaborate.*

Here's your opening, Carl . . . Flutey, here it is . . . ordinary people going about their . . . rope makers . . . eh? Those ropemakers in Boston . . . I'm going to read you a poem I got here, somewhere here . . . Daniel . . . Boston 1776.

Patting his pockets, putting on his spectacles, searching for his poem while he talks, not finding it at once.
Then a thought striking him.

No!
No, here's your opening, this man,
exterior night, this *man* lying on the
grass, from his point of view, he
can't see a thing but grass, dressed
in smallclothes, nothing else,
waistcoat, smallclothes, he's lying
there and he's exhausted,
and there are others like him lying in
the grass, we see them lying there, hear
them lying there.
music, we hear music in the distance, on
the wind, baroque music . . . we hear the
the clang of a ship's bell . . .

MICKEY/PAT: Ding the dong, baby!

JOHN BEAN: . . . we hear drums, they
rattle, tap tap, fifes, we hear fifes,
we hear the *Man in the grass,* him,
he whistles under his breath,
clunk, the sound of digging, clunk,
chunk, the sound of metal on earth,
the sound of a pickaxe, a spade, a
shovel, and murmur, constant murmur of
voices of *Men,* and the *Man in the grass*
stops whistling, he gets up and we come
up with him, up, up with him . . .

JOHN BEAN *whispering, leaning forward, intense, still looking for the poem in his pocket, leaning so far forward that he may be about to fall from his chair.*
But it swings, sweeps him forward and up into the air, above them all.
He is on the boom, the camera boom of a Chapman crane and it sweeps him into the air, his hands coming forward to frame the shot as he goes up.

. . . *Up*! *Up*!
And we see he is not alone, there are
Men with long rifles, with muskets . . .

MICKEY/PAT: Which way to the war, Pop!

JOHN BEAN: . . . they dig, on this hill which
overlooks the harbour of Boston 1776,
titles over, titles, hundreds of *Men* dig,
we see the lights of the British,
a Man-of-war, the ships of the Royal Navy,
we hear the music of the British,
Purcell . . . we hear Purcell and *Main Title*
Over, Purcell, they're dancing in Boston
and these *Men* are digging for their lives,
hundreds of them, and more coming
through the streets of Charlestown,
who are they? what do they do here
digging? how come they are here this
night? Sub Title: Boston, Bunker Hill 1776 . . .

SY HOELMERSBAGGER: Five . . .

JOHN BEAN: What?

MICKEY/PAT: Five five five five . . .

SY HOELMERSBAGGER: Seventeen hundred and seventy-five . . . not important . . .

JOHN BEAN: That's what I want from you, Harvard Man . . .

SY HOELMERSBAGGER: Yale . . . not important.

JOHN BEAN: Right . . Bunker Hill 1776 . . .

SY HOELMERSBAGGER: Breeds Hill . . . not important . . .

JOHN BEAN: . . . *Cut*!

MICKEY/PAT: *Cut*!

JOHN BEAN: . . . *Cut*!
. . . to *Concord*!
Exterior.
Night.
Marching Men . . . *Cut*!
. . . to *Trenton*!
Exterior.
Night.
Marching Men . . . *Cut*!
. . . to *Marblehead*!
Exterior.
Night.
Marching Men . . . *Cut*!
. . . to *Lexington*!
Exterior.
Night.
Marching Men . . . *Cut*!
. . . to Salem, to Philadelphia . . .

MICKEY/PAT: Cut!

JOHN BEAN: . . . to New York!

MICKEY/PAT: Cut!

JOHN BEAN: . . . to Princeton!

MICKEY/PAT: Cut!

JOHN BEAN: . . . to Albany!

MICKEY/PAT: Cut!

MICKEY/PAT *are whooping, hysterical with laughter, tearing off their shirts, to prance near naked like Red Indian braves.*

Whoop whoop . . . we're with you, John!

JOHN BEAN: To Providence, to Springfield, to Reading, to Rhode Island, to the forests, to the plantations, to the mountains: Exterior. Night. Marching Men!

The sound of fife and drum and hammer heard approaching playing 'Yankee Doodle'. JOHN BEAN *puts on his glasses and fumbles again in his pocket for the poem.*

I want to read you . .

SIR FLUTE: Adams!

JOHN BEAN: What?

SIR FLUTE: That was his name . . . not important . . . Frank.

SY HOELMERSBAGGER: Sam . . . not important.

SIR FLUTE: Oh but it is important to me you see . . . Frank.

JOHN BEAN: What?

He has found his poem, a folded scrap of paper, he reads:

'*America* with just *disdain,*
Will break *degenerate* Britain's chain,
And *gloriously* aspire;
I see New *Lockes* and *Camdens* rise,
Whilst other *Newtons* read the skies,
And other *Miltons* wake the lyre.'

Fife and drum and hammer joined by rasp of wielded saw.

'Behold her blazing flag *unfurl'd*,
To awe and rule the western *world*.'

MICKEY/PAT *are gathering together the pencils and paper, they build a little pyre.*

'And teach presumptions *kings*,
Though lull'd by servile flattery's dream,
The *People* are alone *supreme*,
From whom dominion *springs*!'

Silence.
Just sawing.
JOHN BEAN *stands aloft with his hands clasped in front of him, the poem flutters to the floor,* JOHN BEAN *standing head bowed as if in prayer.*
The clonk/thud of a piece of wood falling to the floor as the sawing stops.

JOHN BEAN: Carl? Daniel?

CARL DORF: No.

Exit CARL DORF.
Followed by worried JOE VERIATO.

JOE VERIATO: Come on Carl . . . come on.

Exit JOE VERIATO.

DANIEL RASHUR: Well . . .

Everybody waits on his word.

I am just fooling around with my pencil and I have developed a pretty important thing . . .
I mean the partnership we have here, with the Film Institute of the United Kingdom . . .
Well, if we put them together, the initials I mean . . . we get F.I.U.S. and we get F.I.U.K.

Re-enter JOE VERIATO.

Does anyone see any significance in this?
You know what I mean? I mean Fius Fiuk!

Exit DANIEL RASHUR *good naturedly.*
Followed by worried JOE VERIATO.

JOE VERIATO: Now Dan . . .

Exit JOE VERIATO.
Whoops of joy from MICKEY/PAT.

SIR FLUTE: Do you know, he was the first person to call us a nation of shopkeepers? Adams?
Sam, not Frank, everybody thinks it was Napoleon but it wasn't . . . not Frank, he never said anything much, he was deep, he only bobbed to the surface when he was flushed . . .

Re-enter JOE VERIATO.
Enter WESLEY *with fire extinguisher.*

JOE VERIATO: I want to shake you by the hand . . . do you mind if I call you John?

WESLEY: Dan, I am deeply disturbed by what we may have gotten into here . . .

MICKEY/PAT *gleefully add the poem to the pyre they have built.*
JOHN BEAN *swoops down on the crane, saying to* WESLEY:

JOHN BEAN: Wesley . . . what do you know about the operation of a crane?

WESLEY: I don't think I need to know anything . . .

JOHN DEAN: It's quite simple, Wesley, let me tell you . . . we got it on a counterweight to take our weight . . . so when I step off it means we either have to
change the weights we got, or we have to ask somebody else of the same weight to step on,
now how much do you weigh, Wesley . . .

JOE VERIATO: Get on the crane, Wsley.

WESLEY: I don't think it's any part of . . . I am going to go on a program of weight reduction . . .

JOHN BEAN: Let me ask you not to, son.

WESLEY: I'm going to have to.

JOHN BEAN: Let me tell you, I can't get off unless you get on, Wesley . . . if I get off now, well . . . zonk, up they go, camera and crew . . . zonk!

JOE VERIATO: Get on the crane, Wesley!

WESLEY: No.

JOHN BEAN: Joe . . . now Joe I'll need seventy-five per cent of the producer's

profits . . . Flutey, I want you to
write it . . . Joe, don't look so worried,
we'll go the route I promise you,
on schedule and under budget . . . Joe,
Sir Flute we'll call it 'Washington',
and we'll preview it in the Middle West
to see if it's got *legs*!

Exit JOHN BEAN.

MICKEY/PAT: Get on the crane,
Wesley!

They shout as JOHN BEAN *steps off.*
WESLEY *leaps for the crane, and is plucked skywards.*
Sound of fife, drum and hammers.
JOE VERIATO *torn between his exasperation at* WESLEY *and wanting to follow* JOHN BEAN.

JOE VERIATO: Come down off there,
Wesley.

Exit JOE VERIATO.

MICKEY/PAT: Hey Joe!

Re-enter JOE VERIATO.

We ignited a flame here . . .

Exit MICKEY/PAT as flames leap up from the pyre of pencils.

WESLEY: Oh my God!

A jet of water from on high, douses the pyre.
Curtain

Intermezzo

4 The Curtain rises.
Sound of fife and drums and hammers.
Enter TRIO *of musicians at the head of an* ARMY OF GRIPS. *The* GRIPS *carry saws, timber, hammers, drills, yards of tripe, muskets, flags, skips full of costumes.*
They are under the control of a GAFFER *who squirts a fire extinguisher on the already dead pyre.*

House lights up.

While the ARMY OF GRIPS *goes about its task of transporting us to Ireland where the film set for the Battle of Bunker Hill is being erected the* TRIO *of* DRUMS *and* FIFE *entertains.*

They play a medley of airs, marching and countermarching to the strains of 'Yankee Doodle', 'The Girl I Left Behind Me', 'Lilliburlero', 'Britons Strike Home', 'British Grenadiers', 'The World Turned Upside Down' and back to 'Yankee Doodle'.

They are dressed as the other GRIPS, *with the usual dangling accoutrements depending on trade. A young man plays one drum, an old white-haired man plays the other drum, a middle-aged man plays the fife. As they march and play, the* ARMY *of toiling* GRIPS *sing the songs and do their best to maim or cripple the marching* TRIO. *Planks are thrust out to trip, swing out to brain, nails are left as traps, the ground is littered with hazards which the* TRIO *sidestep neatly never faltering in their music.*

They finish, limping slightly to cheers from dispersing GRIPS *over the ramp of the constructed hill, grass following them as they disappear.*

The music of fife and drums fades.

ACT TWO

The Scene: Location in Ireland for Bunker Hill sequence of 'Washington', circa 1976

1 Exterior. Night. Green grass, a dark sky with stars in it, the stars twinkle, over ramparts and over the bulwarks of men-of-war at anchor in the harbour, over bastions, over hastily constructed earthworks, over ramps, ballrooms, lit by shafts of steel blue, by spurts of flickering candle, lick of wind soaring flame, burst of powder, bedrooms, over filled and filling of gambions, over boats with muffled rowlocks, over flash of dark lantern, over marching men, over sound of drum and fife.

Or, alternatively: an empty stage.

In every Sony eye of every twinkling star, the purple of technicolor and the purple of sound, the voices of passion, intrigue, honour, glory and glory be, the voices of battle and boudoir, talking, urging, declaiming, debating, talking one to the other, one over the other, one under the other, one in spite of the other, the voices of G. P. HUNTLEY JR, LAURENCE OLIVIER, HENRY FONDA, GARY COOPER, ROBERT YOUNG, ROBERT MORLEY, ROBERT BENCHLEY, LESLIE HOWARD, CHARLES LAUGHTON, CEDRIC HARDWICKE, C. AUBREY SMITH, GEORGE ARLISS, HENRY WILCOXON, ROBERT RYAN, LAURENCE OLIVIER, CLAUDETTE COLBERT, BASIL RATHBONE, SPENCER TRACY, GEORGE ARLISS, FREDRIC MARCH, RAYMOND MASSEY, LILIAN HARVEY, DOUGLAS FAIRBANKS JR, MONTAGU LOVE, LIONEL BARRYMORE, WARD BOND, FRANCHOT TONE, LAURENCE OLIVIER AND LAURENCE OLIVIER, ROBERT DONAT, LORETTA YOUNG, RONALD COLMAN, DAVID NIVEN, PETER WILLES, CLIVE BROOK, HENRY FONDA, TYRONE POWER, BETTE DAVIS, GEORGE SANDERS, LAURENCE OLIVIER AND MICHAEL REDGRAVE AND STEWART GRANGER AND FLORA ROBSON AND HENRY FONDA AND LORETTA YOUNG AND LAURENCE OLIVIER AND FREDRIC MARCH AND RAYMOND MASSEY AND GEORGE ARLISS AND LAURENCE OLIVIER.

'What our country needs in its hour
stout hearts and honest decent God-
fearing unhand me sir I beg of you
or I shall be forced to cut you
down where you stand sir by your
leave 'pon my soul but you're a
treacherous rogue, treacherous wretch
have you no honour teach you a lesson
them a lesson him a lesson Parliament
King Country Colony Majesty but a
poor man my sword at your side
your words are bolder than your heart
your actions give the lie to your
your Country is at war
your Government is behind you sire
excellency my lord my dear my word
your heart to forgive me stand fast
you rogues give me a regiment give me
a hundred men give me a chance to
redeem give me a kiss just one let me
kiss those lips dare I kiss those
should I not return
a lock of hair next my heart
thy face in every campfire's flame,
the way is clear
you have fought bravely and no man
can deny that
coward poltroon peasant farmer's boys
pack of cowards under the flag of a
tyrant put up your sword sir
accept my sword sir
keep thy sword sir
had I a sword sir . . .

Or, alternatively it has been recited by the ARMY OF GRIPS *who have marched and countermarched up and over the ramp, at first a straggle of civilians, then wearing bits and pieces of costume, then for a final appearance, with the* TRIO OF FIFE AND DRUM *dressed as the famous patriotic painting 'The Spirit of '76' they are divided into* CIVILIAN/CONTINENTAL ARMY *in mixture of hunting shirts, civilian clothes and militia coats with liberty or death caps, the rudiments*

of uniform as worn by minute-men and Provincial Alarm companies; and soldiers of line regiments of the British Army, very smartly dressed REDCOATS *and behaving as if they know it, with colours and spontoons and halberds and full equipment.*
The BRITISH ARMY *line the route and jeer the raggle taggle of* AMERICA.
Then, exit TRIO.
Exeunt OMNES.

2 Enter JOHN BEAN *wrapped in a cloak to find a shaft of blue in which to stand and brood, the music dying as watches the ships in the harbour.*
Enter JOE VERIATO *to join him.*
They stand in silence a while, the sound of a ship's bell is heard.
JOE VERIATO *thrusts out his hand to shake* JOHN BEAN'S *hand.* JOHN BEAN *grabs it and holds it between his two hands, saying softly:*

JOHN BEAN: I am afraid, Joe.

JOE VERIATO: I don't believe that, John.

JOHN BEAN: I want you to believe it.

JOE VERIATO: If I thought that . . .

JOHN BEAN: Aren't you afraid, Joe?

JOE VERIATO: No, I'm not.

JOHN BEAN: No, let me look at you, no I guess you're not.

JOE VERIATO: It's going to be fine, John. I want you to believe that.
I want you to know that. I know we are going to make a truly great motion picture.
I know it.
John, I know it . . .

They both stand in silence looking down the ramp for a long time, then JOE VERIATO *says:*

JOE VERIATO: John, I'm apprehensive.

JOHN BEAN: I'm shivering, huh?

JOE VERIATO: You're cold, huh?

JOHN BEAN: More than that, the cold clammy hand of foreboding has me by the balls . . .

JOE VERIATO: Oh . . .

JOE VERIATO *removes his hand.*

JOHN BEAN: Now is the time the doubts assail one . . .

JOE VERIATO: I'm afraid . . .

JOHN BEAN: So am I . . .

JOE VERIATO: No no . . . I was saying, I'm afraid it is too late for doubts . . . no no I already explained, I'm not afraid John, I'm apprehensive . . .

JOHN BEAN: What do you stand to lose?

JOE VERIATO: I have gone out on a limb for you . . . I know I've done the right thing, I know you're the one to lead us, I know it, but . . . don't ask me what I've got to lose as if I have nothing to lose . . . come on John, I am associated with you now, wholly associated in every way, we're in this together . . .

JOHN BEAN: I can't let you jump off the wall, Joe . . . I want you to relinquish your rights to your own cut . . .

JOE VERIATO: John, this night of all nights I wish you hadn't asked me that, I must tell you unequivocally the Film Institute of the United States has got to have the final cut.

JOHN BEAN: You would do that to me?

JOE VERIATO: I have to, John.

JOHN BEAN: You are sending me into battle here without my balls, Joe, you have chopped off my balls, Joe.

JOE VERIATO: I haven't done that.

JOHN BEAN: My balls, Joe.

JOE VERIATO: No.

JOHN BEAN: Yes.

JOE VERIATO: No, John . . . no *No*!

JOHN BEAN: Yes, yes . . .

JOE VERIATO: You are working for the Film Institute of the United States, John, you have to go along with what we ask . . .

JOHN BEAN: You are tying my hands behind my back . . .

JOE VERIATO: We don't want to do

anything like that.
We really don't.

JOHN BEAN: I've got a good team.

JOE VERIATO: That's right.

JOHN BEAN: What are they going to say when the know that I don't have final cut?

JOE VERIATO: They don't need to know.

JOHN BEAN: They can smell it.

JOE VERIATO: Let me interject a little reality here . . . so?

JOHN BEAN: So, can I rely on them?

JOE VERIATO: They love you, John.

JOHN BEAN: Am I worthy of that love?

JOE VERIATO: Sure you are. Did you get your script?

JOHN BEAN: Yes.

JOE VERIATO: Did you like the cover?

JOHN BEAN: Yes.

JOE VERIATO: It needs cutting, John.

JOHN BEAN: I agree.

JOE VERIATO: Okay.

JOHN BEAN: It needs a polish, Joe.

JOE VERIATO: I agree.
I made a few cuts, do you want to hear what I cut?

JOHN BEAN: I would be grateful.

JOHN VERIATO: You would?

JOHN BEAN *nods solemnly.* JOE VERIATO *is astonished. He says, after a long time.*

I am afraid, John.

JOHN BEAN: You too?

JOE VERIATO: Me too.

They stand in silence for a long time again. The ship's bell heard again.

JOHN BEAN: It is awesome, that which we embark on . . . truly, let us commend our souls to God . . .

JOE VERIATO: Are you a believer, John?

JOHN BEAN: I am, Joe.

JOE VERIATO: Oh, I find that touching.

JOHN BEAN: It sustains me.

JOE VERIATO: I appreciate that.

JOHN BEAN: Do you know Mahler? Are you sympathetic towards Mahler . . . do you know I heard his third symphony at this moment?

JOE VERIATO: I hear it also, John.

JOHN BEAN: Good.

JOE VERIATO: Do you want me to ask them to turn it down?

JOHN BEAN: No, let them take what pleasure they can this night . . .

JOE VERIATO: I find it full of mood.

JOHN BEAN: Yes.

JOE VERIATO: I guess some of the crew have a musical ear.

JOHN BEAN: They are intelligent and sensitive men, hand-picked men, they have sustained me before . . . I am as nothing without my staff.

JOE VERIATO: Surely.
And what are they without you?

JOHN BEAN: They get by, Joe, believe me they get by . . . one of them has a hostelry in Spain . . .

JOE VERIATO: Is that so?

JOHN BEAN: He is a very wealthy man, yet he comes when I call.

JOE VERIATO: Do I know him?

JOHN BEAN: You ought to, you hired him. Let me tell you something, Joe, know your people, know everything about them and they will go to the ends of the earth for you, my focus puller has come out of retirement for me, paid his own fare and came to me saying: 'How can you go without me, sir?'

JOE VERIATO: That is incredible.
But I am not astonished that you inspire such loyalty.

JOHN BEAN: Well he's pretty broke . . .

JOE VERIATO: We should refund . . . we should pay his first-class ticket . . .

JOHN BEAN: I don't think so, he's not a first-class focus puller.

JOE VERIATO: Oh . . .

JOHN BEAN: He's the first weak link in the chain.

JOE VERIATO: Can we afford to have any weak links?

JOHN BEAN: You've got me, Joe . . .

JOE VERIATO: But you are our strength, John . . . we can afford a weak focus puller, but . . .

JOHN BEAN: We can?

JOE VERIATO: If we've got to have weak links, let one of them be the focus puller . . . but you . . . holy shit, you are our strength.

JOHN BEAN: I am a weak man.

JOE VERIATO: I have a medical report for the purposes of insurance states you are as strong as an ox, you have the heart of a lion . . .

JOHN BEAN: Which veterinarian did you go to?

JOE VERIATO: Come on, John. You're joshing me . . .

JOHN BEAN: I am not.

JOE VERIATO: Well . . . I'm glad you liked your cover . . .

JOHN BEAN: Cover?

JOE VERIATO: Your personalised cover for your copy of the script . . . I know a real craftsman in Sackville Steet, I get them leather bound in Morocco leather, it's tax-deductable . . . hey, did we spell your name right?

JOHN BEAN: It's a simple man, Joe, I'm a simple man with a simple name which is respected throughout the world . . .

JOE VERIATO: Hey, I was merely jesting.

JOHN BEAN: Is this a time for jesting?

JOE VERIATO: Oh come now . . . I've got to chide you . . . oh come now, we have got to keep our sense of humour intact.

JOHN BEAN: Can you get a cloak?

JOE VERIATO: Pardon me?

JOHN BEAN: Can you get a cloak from costume?

JOE VERIATO: I don't understand . . .

JOHN BEAN: Do you want to get a cloak from costume and walk through the tents with me?

JOE VERIATO: You mean incognito?

JOHN BEAN: I think so . . . why not?

JOE VERIATO: Which tents are these, John?
I understand the allusion, but which tents are these?

JOHN BEAN: Costume, make-up, special effects . . . our troops, Joe.

JOE VERIATO: I think they'll know who we are, John.

JOHN BEAN: I hope so, I'm after reassurance not truth . . .

Exit JOHN BEAN *down the ramp, leaving* JOE VERIATO *alone.*
Enter WESLEY.

WESLEY: Joe.

JOE VERIATO: Wesley.

WESLEY: What have we gotten into here?

JOE VERIATO: Wesley, that is the last time I want to hear you say that.
It really is.
We have reached a point where to hear you say such a thing is . . . to hear you ask such a question is . . . I don't want to hear it. What we have gotten into is something special and it is going to . . .
You Wesley, you are . . .
Wesley, what have you done with your life? Here is an opportunity for you to . . .
You can shine, Wesley.

WESLEY: It is going to be so disastrous.

JOE VERIATO: It is not.

WESLEY: Everybody is so convinced. It is the most horrendous script . . .

JOE VERIATO: It is not.

WESLEY: I have read it Joe.

JOE VERIATO: Do you think I haven't?

WESLEY: We are all going to die.

JOE VERIATO: We are not.

WESLEY: Right up to the last moment I hoped . . . but I have seen nothing, all we have left is . . . what have we left, Joe?

JOE VERIATO: One of the finest directors in the world, Wesley.

WESLEY: It is so boring, the script is so boring, it's just boring, everybody is going to be so bored.

People are bored at this moment, at this very moment, people who haven't even read the script are bored. I want you to come with me and talk to people, professional people . . . I've been talking to everybody, and they are convinced that they are involved in the most boring film they have ever been involved in. They have no faith in John Bean, they say that his last five films have been so boring . . . his last *five*! They know, they've all worked on them, they are loyal persons, but they are all yawning at the prospect of tomorrow . . .

JOE VERIATO: It's late at night. At this time of night people yawn legitimately, with the best of intentions . . . try as I may, I am yawning at the very sound of the word . . . it works that way . . . you are yawning . . .

WESLEY: I know.

JOE VERIATO: It has a snowballing effect.

WESLEY: I know.

JOE VERIATO: People yawn when they are apprehensive.
Frightened . . . they have a right to be frightened, apprehensive, we're all . . . I'm tired.

WESLEY: We can still pull out.

JOE VERIATO: No, *no*!
We need the credits.

WESLEY: What the hell is my credit going to be?

JOE VERIATO: The Film Institute of the United States needs the credits. Not you . . . you'll get a credit, you are Personal Assistant to Mr Bean . . .

WESLEY: I don't want to be.

JOE VERIATO: He has chosen you. You are the right size and the right weight.

WESLEY: I am not, I am too heavy.

JOE VERIATO: He has put on weight also.
Don't you understand how lucky you are to be so close to . . . we are about to be tested, all of us, there are some among us who are cowards, some rogues, some phonies, some drunks,
Christ we must surely have every kind of frailty and human weakness, but be assured there are brave men also,
this is so perfectly as it was perhaps, you know what I mean?
God knows . . . right?
I am ready to be tested. I want to put myself into the arena, you know what I mean, I shudder, but I go forth.

WESLEY: We can still pull out.

JOE VERIATO: I can give you leave to go.

WESLEY: Thank you.

JOE VERIATO: You'll regret it.

WESLEY: No, I won't.

JOE VERIATO: When you see the movie, you'll regret it.

WESLEY: I don't think so.

JOE VERIATO: You were not with us.

WESLEY: I really don't think so.

JOE VERIATO: What will you say?

WESLEY: I don't have to say anything.

JOE VERIATO: Then you may go . . . you can obviously reconcile your decision in your own mind.

WESLEY: I think so.

JOE VERIATO: Those who are not with us are against us.

WESLEY: I am against you.

JOE VERIATO: God forgive you.

WESLEY: I don't believe in God.

JOE VERIATO: Then we don't want you.

WESLEY: I know you don't, but if I go

who is going to oppose you?

JOE VERIATO: Nobody is going to oppose me.

WESLEY: That's right.

JOE VERIATO: Why should anybody want to oppose me?

WESLEY: You are doing the wrong thing.

JOE VERIATO: Is that your considered artistic judgement?

WESLEY: Everything tells me that we are hellbent on disaster here.

JOE VERIATO: Then I ask you to go, in God's name . . . go!

WESLEY: No . . . and you can't make me. I was appointed by the Film Institute of the United States . . . no, I'm going to stay.

JOE VERIATO: Are you going to be a divisive influence?

WESLEY: From the moment that shooting starts I am going to be as loyal as the next man . . . you will have no cause to complain of my conduct.

JOE VERIATO: Very well.

WESLEY: When I do oppose you, and I shall do so, it will be on matters which I shall record and have witnessed as being contrary to the artistic integrity of
the motion picture like a lousy fucking script . . .

JOE VERIATO: Come on Wesley . . .

WESLEY: Like the decision to cast Mary Jane Pendejo as Tarleton . . .

JOE VERIATO: He was a very well . . . he was beautiful, you've seen the painting, he had the most fantastic legs, it's a satire, Wesley . . .
He had incredible thighs, we couldn't find a male star with such thighs . . . she only has to wave.
I know . . . I know we didn't want it to become a vehicle, but some people have a right to be in this film you know, some people have suffered tyranny,
my father was humiliated because of his background, my grandparents were three months on Ellis Island . . . Mary Jane Pendejo was forced to work in a brothel when she was a child, she has a right to a place in this movie . . . and she couldn't play Martha now could she? She only has to wave and order the massacre of Waxhaws, that's all.

WESLEY: There is no massacre at Waxhaws in the script . . .

JOE VERIATO: Sir Flute is at this very moment hacking that . . .

WESLEY: Is it going to come before or during Bunker Hill . . . ?

JOE VERIATO: It's going to come where John Bean wishes it to come.

WESLEY: Because it didn't happen until a good two years afterwards.

JOE VERIATO: I know that.

WESLEY: Why can't she play Jane McCrea?

JOE VERIATO: We've gone into that.

WESLEY: She could do that, all she's got to do is lose her hair, she ought
to enjoy that . . . she can lose everything
the way she usually does and then can
come the ultimate, she can lose her hair,
the ultimate sexual cinematic experience
topless, bottomless, hairless,
and all that blood . . . we'll call the
freak who scalps her Red Wings,
maybe he can ride a primitive motor cycle,
I don't know . . . that would be something,
that really would be something,
you know, the scalp of Jane McCrea from
his aerial and you know Gentleman Johnny
sees it and says, 'Shit, Red Wings you goofed . . . we have lost the war.'

JOE VERIATO: What is there of value in this diatribe, Wesley?

WESLEY: I have asked for an investigation.

JOE VERIATO: I know.

WESLEY: Sy Hoelmersbagger and Dan Rashur are flying out.

JOE VERIATO: I welcome them as fellow Fellows of the Film Institute of the United States.
With joy.
Where have you accommodated them,

Wesley?
I don't think they should be in
Waterford,
I think they should be here with us,
under the stars, about to face the might
of England, coming up that hill, Wesley.
Here.

He points dramatically down the hill of timber and grass.

WESLEY: They are empowered to stop the picture, Joe . . .

JOE VERIATO: If they have the muscle.
'Do not step on me!'
More than that, have they considered
the consequences of telling three or
four hundred bloodthirsty savages
that they are fired?
Can they stand up to three or four
hundred redcoated Irish extras and tell
them to disperse to their homes?
If they have the gall, if they have the
guts . . . then I want to see them do it.
Now, I must bid you good night, Wesley,
for there are certain things I have to
do if I am to face the morrow myself
in good heart.

Exit JOE VERIATO *down the hill.*
Enter SECOND ASSISTANT *with call sheets.*

SECOND ASSISTANT: I salute you.

WESLEY: Uh huh.

SECOND ASSISTANT: I come bearing call sheets.

WESLEY: Thank you.

SECOND ASSISTANT: That which we are about to do . . .

WESLEY: Those of us about to die . . .

The SECOND ASSISTANT *hands* WESLEY *a call sheet, his finger pointing to* WESLEY's *name.*
WESLEY *nods.*

Right.

SECOND ASSISTANT: I must point out
to you that you are called at dawn.
Five thirty to be exact.

WESLEY: I know that. I've got to cook his goddam breakfast!

Exit WESLEY *down the hill.*
Exit SECOND ASSISTANT.

3 Enter SIR FLUTE PARSONS *in cloak and cocked hat.*
The far-off sound of fife and drum, and the clang of a ship's bell.
Very little light.
Enter JOHN BEAN *shrouded in a cloak.*
To be challenged by SIR FLUTE:

SIR FLUTE: Hold! Who comes?
Who goes? Who is it? I'm here . . . you
are? Sir, you are?

JOHN BEAN: A friend.

SIR FLUTE: You don't know how happy
it makes me to hear you say that. One
can never be too sure, all these Irish
around, bearing weapons.
Don't want to end up tarred or feathered
at my age if you don't mind.
Are you English at all?

JOHN BEAN: At all?

SIR FLUTE: In any way? I am.
I don't mind admitting it, though I do
keep my voice down in crowded places.
These crowded places. Actually, I am
to all intents and purposes the only
English person here and we came
originally from the Balkans, my family,
very rum lot.
Some pogrom got them fleeing. They
used
to dance on tables at first but we've
managed to live that down . . . actually
there is one other but he is trying to
be a German, I tell him at breakfast
he's as English as I am, loudly, at
breakfast, it makes nim tremble, egg
all down his chin . . . I feel very
brave when I do it, terrified afterwards,
that's the Balkan in me.
He's from Hampstead, but he says he
isn't, of course he is . . . however,
nothing
wrong in that, I can think of a thousand
and one reasons why one should not
mention Hampstead.
As the war progresses, it's going to be
more difficult to be English, I've put a
lot of anti-English into it, anti-British,
anti-eeeeeeeeverything, well . . . one felt
one ought and I've never really had any
integrity about . . . anything, I'm telling
you this because you're a stranger,
because you're clothed in the garb of
night, as it were, I say things like
that quite accidentally,

they aren't attempts at purple, I say
that in case you are a student . . . they
will pin one down so . . . especially
the American ones who are so sweet in
other ways and I've valued it,
one of them said to me that as you get
older you get nicer and he must have
meant
me because he was a child,
but he taught me things, some of them
amazing, a wonderful child, so ingenious
and so understanding and so loving!
Wonderful.
But not entirely called for, I was getting
on quite well before.
Missionary style.
Wesson oil?
Do you know anything about it? I mean,
why?
Well, it ended just the same as usual,
flat . . .
How friendly are you?

JOHN BEAN: I love you.

SIR FLUTE: That's friendly, that's
extraordinarily friendly, I've only said
that to two men my entire life and one of
those was my father.

JOHN BEAN: I love you all.

SIR FLUTE: Now you've spoiled it.

JOHN BEAN *casts off his cloak and goes to gaze down on the reverse slope of the hill.*
SIR FLUTE *recognises him, sighs:*

SIR FLUTE: Oh, it's you . . .
Well I haven't been able to do anything
about that bloody silly Declaration of
Independence scene . . . you can't just
have them whipping out their quills
and signing it then and there,
they didn't, it took weeks, just like
a contract, argy-bargy for weeks and
they took even longer to let everyone
know that they'd done it . . . and it's
wordy.
Well, you'll just have to have lots of
things going on at the same time and
hope that nobody bothers to listen to
the words . . . but we'll think of
something, some way of livening it up,
we haven't done badly so far.
What are you doing wandering about like
that?
I was cold.

JOHN BEAN: Our troops are in good
heart, Sir Flute.

SIR FLUTE: Isn't that marvellous . . .

JOHN BEAN: You?

SIR FLUTE: Me?

JOHN BEAN: Does your spirit falter?

SIR FLUTE: Not at all, not at all,
looking forward to it enormously, it's
going to be outrageous, I haven't stopped
enjoying it all the way through . . . I
don't know how you dare do it, but
you're obviously going through with it
and I feel like a new man, it's
outrageous!

JOHN BEAN: Is it too outrageous?

SIR FLUTE: I don't think so. Is it
outrageous enough?
Have we turned it upside down enough?

JOHN BEAN: Have we turned it upside
down too much?

SIR FLUTE: I don't think so.
What do you think?

JOHN BEAN: I don't know. I just don't
know.

SIR FLUTE: No, I don't know. Is there
enough action for you?

JOHN BEAN: I think so.

SIR FLUTE: Oh good, because I'm not
good at that . . . too much do you think,
have I overcompensated, stuck everybody
on a horse when it would be better they
stood still?

JOHN BEAN: I think we need action.

SIR FLUTE: Oh good, and what about
the language, we didn't want 'gadzooks'
and all that did we?
Too anachronistic, do you think?

JOHN BEAN: I think the trouble goes
deeper than that . . .

SIR FLUTE: It does?

JOHN BEAN: Yes, I think so. I don't
think you believe in the American
Revolution, you don't believe it . . .

SIR FLUTE: Oh it happened, oh yes,
that was the first thing I found out.

JOHN BEAN: I am deeply serious.

SIR FLUTE: So too am I . . .

JOHN BEAN: You are?

SIR FLUTE: Well, I'm beginning to be.

JOHN BEAN: I'm very happy to hear that.

SIR FLUTE: Oh come now, where would we
all be without America? We all need
America desperately . . . I know I do
and I wish you well, all of you, you've
managed to do it, I think you have,
and we've always been awful about you,
an awful amount of condescension,
well, you say such awful things sometimes
but so do we and we're not getting any
better whereas I believe you are,
getting better I mean, have got better
I mean, will get better and better
even though you have made the most
awful mistakes, awful . . . I'm not talking
about Vietnam which was all the rage not
so long ago, nor Watergate, I mean we
could all have done that, goodness how
we did do that, this war we are about
to fire the first few shots in has a
lot in it very silly,
and we're going to have such fun with
it, the silly things in it,
but you know there aren't that many
silly things, what you did was quite
quite wonderful and I don't mean the
fact that you won,
no no, though that was nice, for you,
and you see ultimately for us . . . it's
to do with people you see, the people
thing . . . oh good lord Sam Adams was
a bit of a humbug and an awfully dangerous
man for you as much as us, don't you think?
well, perhaps not . . . but you said it you
see, you said all that pretentious rights
of man nonsense and then went and did it,
of course you got a lot of help from
Englishmen, I mean Tom Paine, and a lot
of it was lip service, and you have got
the black people who have been a bit of a
problem for you, but you've learned from
your mistakes you see,
have we? We don't seem to have, not
an awful lot, we don't care quite so
much about freedom as you do, do we?
The freedom of the individual? Do we?
I'm sure we don't, look at the way
we're taxed, I'm taxed out of all
existence, it's only by working for
people like you that I'm able to live
at all, by the way that we can arrange
things, a little here and a little there
and a tiny bit in a Swiss bank,
it's so . . . so . . . free, do you see?
If you hadn't won, who would we be
working for now?
I'm ridiculously grateful to you and
your Revolution, taught us a lesson you
see . . . of course we went on and did even
better for a while without you, but what
about that marvellous music you've given
us, would we have had that? I doubt it,
we threw our black people off our
conscience such a long time ago and all
we got was steel bands and calypso,
which was a little sad, because we had
treated them quite badly, obviously not
badly enough, needed more than that to
produce a really solid contribution,
and now you all do it don't you, white
and black, possibly white more than black,
jitterbugging . . . I used to be able to,
I do have a natural grace in the same way
that many of you don't,
but it isn't an English characteristic
on the whole, wish it was, so there you
are . . . you've done awfully well and we
wouldn't have you different, and we're
awfully glad we lost, isn't it time we
started to enjoy some of the fruits of
defeat . . . perhaps we did at the time,
we got India and look what that's done for
Bradford, transformed it . . . very exciting.

You were so marvellous during the war. You
know that line I have Lord Howe say about
'effeminate things, unfit for and
impatient of war' meaning Americans, well,
he didn't say it actually but why shouldn't
he, he's our villain after all? I got
such a marvellous memory flooding back
into me of the last war, in London and
these two marvellous young men,

beautiful young men . . . gosh they were
such a relief after our shaven-headed
clumpers, they were a delight . . . and
then they vanished,
we were all sad when you went off like
that and then we read the newspapers
and
were so grateful . . . though what these
boys thought of it I don't know and you
did have some brutes . . .

Does that convince you?

I think you have the secret, I think
you discovered it then, and I think we
lost it . . . thank you for so often
allowing
me to share in it, I would hate to have to
be a Russian, they would never
understand me
and I would consequently not last five
minutes . . . so, I do believe in your
Revolution, so much nicer than
everybody
else's.

The secret of eternal youth I mean,
spotty,
vicious, but often gentle and sometimes
kind . . . look at how you've poured
money
into everybody's pocket and still do,
of course you want us to perform for
you,
and we do . . . I hope well, I hope with
dignity, and I'm sure you'd be the first
to tell us if we didn't.

Are we doing well? I ask you? Are we
all that you want us to be?

Have we done enough to make up for
the fact
that we were so awful all those years
ago,
I mean we gave you such a good time
during
the war didn't we?

Didn't that help? I know the French had
a hand in it as well, of course, how
you adored Paris, wanted to stay for
ever . . . so unkind, you've always
wanted Paris . . . well we weren't Paris
but we did our best, glad to do it,
we've never been ashamed of anything
like that . . . I mean when we need
something the great thing about us is
that we're the first to up with our
skirts and down with our drawers and
straight to nearest wall, we've always
been best with our backs to the wall,
everybody says so, fourpence and find
your own wall, Yank . . . yes I think we
did give you a good if rather short
time . . . but, first day of shooting
tomorrow and can I have it in cash
in a suitcase, in dollars?

That which I'm owed for my services
so that I may buzz off and leave you to
the good work . . . off with a clear
conscience having done all that I've
been asked without embarrassment,
without
shame, without argument, without
conviction
but you wouldn't expect that from me.

Would you?

Yes, you obviously would, well . . . well,
the marvellous thing about your excuse
for a Revolution is that it wasn't one
at all . . . hardly noticed when all was
said and done, hard-headed business
men who very sensibly used what they
needed
and then got on with it as freemen,
wonderfully free . . . that's what we all
remember, and we're all grateful to you,
it could have been so much worse,
look at
how the French behaved, even to poor
old
Tom Paine . . . which only goes to show
you shouldn't be a revolutionary if you
can't take a joke.

Are you going to say anything?

Haven't I said everything you want
to hear? I hope I have.

I hope I always do that, I'm not much
use
to you if I don't . . . I would rather be
out of the way before the shooting starts,
the actual shooting . . . I shall leave you
a phone number in France,
you see there have been such rumours . . .
Are they true?

JOHN BEAN *doesn't answer. He has
wrapped himself in his cloak again
and watches the light changing from
blue of night to steel of dawn, a
wisp of mist.*

SIR FLUTE: They can't be . . . even
you wouldn't be mad enough to give

them real bullets.
Would you?

4 'The First and Last Day of Shooting.' Enter GAFFER *with a bacon roll in one hand and plastic cup of steaming coffee in the other.*
SIR FLUTE *shivers, huddles himself in his cloak.*

SIR FLUTE: Awfully cold. Then Ireland so often is . . .

GAFFER: His focus puller is pissed.

SIR FLUTE: Oh dear.

GAFFER: Oh yes.

SIR FLUTE: It's in a worthy cause.

GAFFER: Is it?

SIR FLUTE: He's a wonderful director and he's got a first-rate script.

GAFFER: Has he?

SIR FLUTE: Oh to be sure. Don't you think so? Aren't you proud to be with him this day? He's going to make a marvellous film about a marvellous and very important subject, you'll all be famous and your fees will rocket so high you'll be too expensive to ever be employed again . . . but you stick out for your money, I always do . . .

JOHN BEAN: I would rather never work again and do this motion picture with this *Director,* this *Man*, at this moment of time. If I should die this day I know that I die with a *Director* who goes forward on a just and honourable and an important project.

GAFFER: Sure that's more than we know.
Sure it is . . .
That's right. And more than we to know, if you follow me, sure . . . begorrah, Christ save us. We are, I am, we are working for him and I do not give a monkey's
fuck . . . if he says I should do this or do that or use his shit for toothpaste then I shall, Jesus, without any fuss at all, at all . . . and if he fucks it up sure who is to blame but him,
all we have to say is that we did our part, as we were *directed* to do,
by the *Director* and no man can put it down
to me anyway in the least . . . I being only
the Gaffer to the Grips, this day . . .

Sure I shan't lose any sleep this day over whether this day, the *Man* is getting into good or not so good or very bad this day, what his intentions are this day, honourable or not this day . . .

SIR FLUTE: Ah, but if the intention is not
good, what of those that are ruined this day? Their reputations spoiled, the actors of this day, those that are discard, cut, coils on the floor, snicks and clips, half a performance here,
a line there,
a word here, a section of superb gaffering gone unremarked, arms legs heads and badly
lit bedroom parts, when all these,
all they, when all they join up and cry, 'We died that day in Ireland', some swearing transatlantic oaths,
some crying for a surgeon to put their parts back together,
some upon their newest wives left poor behind them, for they will never work again, some upon their children left to suffer insult at their fathers thus rawly offered in later years on television, for even though they may perform well and give what they have there is often that about the *Direction* of a performance can taint and dismember and dishonour and the death of an actor follows on the first showing and the showing and the late night showing, though he himself died that day he dies again a thousand times on the showing . . . even though he has tried his utmost, and those that strove with him are honoured and long contracted for seven films . . . yet may he be dead.

And I am afeared that there are few die well who die in motion pictures,
for how can they be charitably viewed who die in battle when money was the argument?

Now if these men who die, do not die well
it will be a black matter for the *Director* who directed them . . .

JOHN BEAN: I don't think so.

SIR FLUTE: You don't? I hope I

pasticed it properly . . .
You don't?

JOHN BEAN: No. For no director can know that which will be the cause of success or failure to his actors and all those strive with *Him* to come to that good effect, *Success*! What if they are up to now steady and sober and truly professional yet teeter on the brink of ghastly crime, like losing a day, like being so stoned he cannot sit a horse . . . though how often have I . . . has this *Man* been called upon to cover by light and angle and re-scheduling been called upon to cover up such crimes which can throw budgets in a loop? and lose the trust of friends . . . how many times has *Our Director* taken good care to avoid the droop of last nights debauch in an eye, the wild panting fever of a sexual neurotic, her pain obvious close but spared derision and contempt by medium long shot which shows her demure though restless, the crab and gouge of age hitherto disclaimed?

ANd how can he know what they do?

Let them answer to God and the front office, and if they die, let them not blame him . . . for I tell you, *He* who would avoid the damnation of his motion picture will not be profligate with the lives of his soldiers, and yet he will not spare them, their duty . . . and will call upon them to die with him, their duty so to do, contracted and witnessed, so they are his . . . but they take their conscience with them when later they are offered work.

So, let the actors come to this day, clean. Let them be shriven of every day lost, every line spoken badly or forgotten, every virgin thought befouled and ravished and trot for others out at a cent a throw, retaken and retaken by sweaty crew, every extra dollar squeezed up front, every first-class fare stretched to accommodate wife, mistress, catamite, and let them not cast blame on *Him*, their *Director* should they know bc guilty of crimes he knows not of . . . and likewise crew, let them not also, let them determine to give their best endeavour, without strikes, without petty quibbles as to hours . . .

GAFFER: I'm sure I'll do my best, but whther I do or I do not, I'll not blame *Him* . . .

JOHN BEAN: And I think I made a fair pastiche myself of it . . .

SIR FLUTE: And I shall not blame him and yet I determine to fight lustily for him, have fought and now would go, paid.

Enter FOCUS FULLER, *old and grey and pissed.*
They all contemplate him. The GAFFER *says sadly as he watches the* FOCUS FULLER *dance a little dance, bacon roll in one hand, bottle in the other:*

GAFFER: And there is the first casualty we have . . . this man plucked from the sanctuary of his health farm where at least he may dream of drink and pulling thc focus of those ladies he has been nearest to, their distance, sucking in his horny breath as they heave in their inches, getting nearer to . . . there, plucked from sanctuary by *Director's* whim, as if there were not focus pullers, plucked from his carrot juice, from his contemplation of his navel and those forbidden parts he has taken his measure to and tossed and groaned lustily at the later remembrance of, now plucked from sanctuary as a child from a nipple, as if there were not focus pullers enough . . . that this one should be taken . . . to be given poison, that which to him is poison, though to us more sturdy is merely mother's milk, Guinness.

Enter GRIPS *armed with bacon rolls and coffee to contemplate the sad dance of the* FOCUS PULLER.

Enter CREW.
The GRIPS *give way at their entrance.*

GAFFER: And when there is Oscars going who is remembered, not me . . . not him poor sot who will never work again.

JOHN BEAN: I myself have heard your . . . our *Director* say he cares not for Oscars unless they are for you all . . .

GAFFER: Oh yes? Sure and fuck it he says many things, many such things to make us work with a will . . . but when it's all over and he is showered with praises I'll doubt he'll do more than . . .

JOHN BEAN: He has more to lose than any here.

GAFFER: That's just rubbish, there are those here have everything to lose . . .

JOHN BEAN: If he forgets those that went into this day with him, I'll never trust his word again . . .

GAFFER: Get you!

JOHN BEAN: Piss off!

GAFFER: I'll kick your fucking teeth in. Or I would if I didn't have work to do, but I'll kick your fucking teeth in afterwards . . .

JOHN BEAN: Well said, there's work to do, you may try afterwards, you may try . . . but how shall I know you?

GAFFER: Know me? How shall I know you? Every fucker knows me, fucking Jesus, everybody knows me . . . the *Director* knows me and I know him, like that we are and that's me on top. What's your fucking name . . . better still who's your fucking agent? I'll kick his fucking teeth in as well.

GRIP: That's it Lou, you smash him.

GAFFER: By Fuck I will . . . !

SIR FLUTE: Be friends you English fools, be friends!

GAFFER: Don't call me a fucking fool, you toffee-nosed cunt . . .

Smash! He hits SIR FLUTE *smartly on the nose, withal.*
SIR FLUTE *goes down. Holding it.*

Stone me, actors!

The GAFFER *loses his appalling Irish accent and resumes his natural East End as he rails.*
The CREW *disdainfully setting up.*

Fucking actors, stone me . . . cheeky buggers, some cheeky fucking actor, hear that lads?

GRIP: That's it Paddy, you tell him.

The FOCUS PULLER *swaying round them all with a childish leer on his face, his bottle which is never empty in his hand, he sings a song without words as he dances, sways. He is ignored by everyone.*
GAFFER *sizes up* JOHN BEAN, *asks him:*

GAFFER: What's your fucking name?

Not that it'll be your real fucking name,
you'll be using some poof name won't you,
know what I mean? Never known an actor
yet called Joe Soap, know what I mean?

Let me know so I can,
when the last inch is in, give it to you,
wham!

Know what I mean?

How many times? Actors . . . how many
times when we've sweat and strained,
forbear from dropping fuck all on 'em,
though Jesus the temptation has been great,
know what I mean,
so tight arsed have they been . . . and then
when you go to see them, my life, no idea!

No idea whatsoever, but I'll leave off,
for any spark may cause a fire,
and he might need your fissog unkicked
in . . . and as I say in this part of the
world where the least thing sparks 'em
off . . . I've took the GB plate off of
my car don't you worry . . . you might be
a mate of some cunt with a mate who's
got a mate don't mind who he mutilates,
so . . . but when it's all over and we're
back in Blighty I shall seek you out and
knock seven colours of shit out of you,
though I've forgotten why,
mostly because you have got on my tits
already raw.

So I'll take your name.

SIR FLUTE *thrusts a card at him, saying:*

SIR FLUTE: Mine is Flute Parsons and this is the name of my lawyer!

GAFFER: I've dealt with you, mate, it's his name I'm after . . .

JOHN BEAN *throws off his cloak to reveal himself as* JOHN BEAN.

JOHN BEAN: My name is John Bean and I forgive you!

GAFFER: Who?

JOHN BEAN: John Bean.

GAFFER: Right, your name is took John Bean and you are due a duffing up soon as we get this in the can . . .

I shall see you bear a charmed life,
no tripe to trip over, no fear of
going through nothing, you shall be given
the gentlest horses, you shall fear
nothing, well lit, well provided for so
that you might give of your best and then
last day of shooting plus a few weeks for
possible retakes I shall come into your
life with hobnail boots . . .

JOHN BEAN: I am your director.

GAFFER: Fuck me, why didn't you say so, I'd have smashed you then and there . . . !

He throws himself at JOHN BEAN *who staggers back under the onslaught.*

If there's one thing worse than actors
it's directors . . . and you may get rid of
me tomorrow.

How dare you to do what you have done,
like you were some kind of God . . .?
Eh?

Kicking the prostrate JOHN BEAN.

For they think they are God, do they not?

But they are not, and even if they were
it would matter little to me,
I am not inclined to listen to God either,
whichever God . . . right, get up and do
your worst, director, but don't creep
about as if you are God in a cloak,
as if we cared, as if it matters whether
we know who you are or not,
we don't give a shit, baby, we'll tell
you how we feel . . . we'll give you the
full strength don't you worry,
you don't need to spy, how dare you think
you should? Eh?

We have never . . . never been walked on
yet by the likes of you, mate,
directors I've shit 'em . . . what did
you say? Eh? 'Shit a few more . . .'
What?
Eh?
'For the British Film Industry needs them . . .'
Eh?
Right, right . . .
Get on with it.
Know what I mean? What do you want?
Quiet!
They're coming . . . hark . . . the drums,
eh?
Come on, you do what you've got to do.
Absolute quiet please.
And you . . .

Shoving SIR FLUTE *forward.*

Come on . . . stand by . . . absolute
quiet if you please . . . and you . . .
Come on, stand by, keep an oyster.
Come on . . .

Tugging JOHN BEAN *to his feet and pointing down the hill.*
The distant sound of fife and drum.

Come on sir, you can do it sir, fully
fledged paid up member like you, sir
. . . let's have some directing, guv, to
that good end, eh?
See here, they are as it were coming up
this hill and dollars mate, for they are
being paid for every step they take, by
the left, dollars, dollars, dollars,
come on then, let's have you, left right
left . . . come on genius!

THE CREW *are sitting on the crane with their camera.*
The SOUND MAN *puts his earphones on.*
The CAMERA OPERATOR *speaks from his perch.*

OPERATOR: All right, genius, you want to make a movie, what's the stop?

GAFFER: Eh? Where is he? Where's the lighting cameraman?

MAURICE: Second Unit, down the hill.

GAFFER: Treacherous bastard, he should be up here with the workers . . .

OPERATOR: All right Trotsy, you want to start, give us the stop . . . I'm anybody's . . .

GAFFER: Bernie. Bernie the Volt, what's the stop?

The GAFFER *squints up at the sky, at the scene, waggles a finger to* BERNIE THE VOLT *who shuffles forward.*
They whisper together. BERNIE *squints up at the sky himself and suggests:*

BERNIE: Stop it down to eleven.

OPERATOR: Eh?

GAFFER: Eleven.

BERNIE: Well . . .

GAFFER: No no . . . make it a gnats under eleven.

OPERATOR: You're joking . . .

BERNIE: No, I tell a lie . . . make it a tweak over a heavy nine five . . .

OPERATOR: That's better, might be able to see something . . . right, ready when you are, sir.

GAFFER: Ready when you are sir, guv, absolute quiet please while the guv'nor climbs aboard . . .

JOHN BEAN *looks at him, at the crane, at the advancing British Army down the hill.*

JOHN BEAN: Okay . . .

GAFFER: Right sir . . .

JOHN BEAN: You want me to shoot this?

GAFFER: Right sir. Keep the noise down.

JOHN BEAN: Okay kid – okay. You don't have any actors.

GAFFER: What's this lot marching up the hill, Fred bleedin' Karno's . . . and this here . . . ?

JOHN BEAN: Okay.

GAFFER: Claw? Camel? Bernie, let's have you? O.K.? Absolute quiet please. Stand by . . . Turnover . . .

JOHN BEAN: Now just a moment . . .

GAFFER: Hold the roll!

MAURICE: Cut it.

GAFFER: Just a moment for the guv'nor . . . sir?

JOHN BEAN: We still have time . . . are you sure?

GAFFER: I am sure. Are you sure, sir?

JOHN BEAN: Sure I'm sure, what am I supposed to be sure about?

GAFFER: Are you sure you can make it look something like, know what I mean? Can you guarantee that the resultant picture will look something like? Keep a choirboy!

To GRIPS *who are shuffling forward to look down the hill at the advancing* BRITISH ARMY.

Know what I mean?

JOHN BEAN: What is it stirs within you, sir? Why is this so important to you? What can the making of this film about the birth of our nation mean to you?
What stirs you, kid?

GAFFER: Work.
The workers will make this film.
And we'll make it now. All right, lads, stand by . . .

JOHN BEAN: This is my film.

GAFFER: Do you have final cut?

JOHN BEAN: No, I do not.

GAFFER: Then it's anybody's film.
Get aboard the crane . . . you . . . you.

SIR FLUTE: Me?

GAFFER: Yes you . . . say your lines.

SIR FLUTE: I don't have any lines.

GAFFER: Where do you want him, guv?

JOHN BEAN: Do I have final cut?

GAFFER: If you make a film for us you get final cut . . .

JOHN BEAN: Then I shall shoot the film.

GAFFER: Where do you want this

geezer?

SIR FLUTE: I am not an actor.

GAFFER: What are you then?

SIR FLUTE: An old gentleman.

GAFFER: What's your name?

SIR FLUTE: Sir Flute Parsons.

GAFFER: Right, just say anything, we'll dub you afterwards . . . make out you're working for some wop, that's all post sync isn't it? Know what I mean? Absolute quiet . . . stand up . . . turn over.

JOHN BEAN: Just one moment.

GAFFER: Yes, sir . . . ?

JOHN BEAN: I don't have Wesley.

GAFFER: Fetch Wesley . . .

Pushing one of the GRIPS *down the hill.*
Then tugging SIR FLUTE *into position on the ridge.*

Stand there, all right, sir?

JOHN BEAN: Who are you supposed to be?

SIR FLUTE: Who am I supposed to be?

GAFFER: Eh? Fucking George Washington aren't you?

SIR FLUTE: I don't think so.
He wasn't at Bunker Hill.

GAFFER: Neither are you, you're in fucking Ireland, stand still and say something.

Enter WESLEY *up the hill.*

WESLEY: Now stop this. Stop this . . . where's Joe . . . he's got to stop this.

JOHN BEAN: Are you with us or against us, Wesley?

WESLEY: I have Dan Rashur and Sy Hoelmersbagger of the Film Institute of the United States with me, down that hill, they are coming up to tell you that they have reached the painful decision that this motion picture must not start shooting this day . . . if you start shooting this day, we will have to pay out a great deal of money, we have to pay the actors, we have to pay the grips, we have to pay the writer . . .

SIR FLUTE: Oh really? Of course, first day of shooting . . . of course . . . Absolutely.
Is it a great deal of money, have you got it with you?

WESLEY: We have no money. We have had financial support withdrawn.

JOHN BEAN: We'll make it without money.

Enter JOE VERIATO *with* HEINRICH GUTTMEIR.

JOE VERIATO: We have backing, John.
We have the backing of the British Government in this, through the Film Institute of the United Kingdom . . . I'd like you to meet Heinrich.

SIR FLUTE: That's my German from Hampstead.

HEINRICH: I'm delighted to meet you, Mr Bean . . . we think it's going to be a very funny film, a very important film, very important for Britain.
we would like it to be the Royal Command Performance Film.

SIR FLUTE: I'm sorry, but I haven't written that kind of film.

GAFFER: There are five hundred jobs at stake here.

HEINRICH: We are aware of this.

WESLEY: I cannot allow this film to be made, I'm sorry.

JOHN BEAN: How are you going to stop us, Wesley?

WESLEY: I don't know.

JOHN BEAN: Join with us, Wesley, I can't get off the crane without you.

WESLEY: No, no I must follow my own convictions in this . . . I'm sorry, I must go back down the hill. We're going to stop you, Joe. We have the rights to your script Sir Flute Parsons. We do not intend to make those rights over to anyone else and we do not intend to allow shooting to start.
We're coming back up the hill and we're going to stop you.

JOHN BEAN: I don't think so.

JOE VERIATO: I would rather have you with us, Wesley . . . but . . .

Exit WESLEY *down the hill.*
JOE VERIATO *watches him go and then says nodding down towards the sound of drum and fife, his arm around* HEINRICH GUTTMEIR's *shoulder:*

JOE VERIATO: Well Heinrich, I guess it's our Irish against their Irish.

GAFFER: Clear the set, Maurice.

MAURICE: Mr Veriato, Mr . . . Mr er um, behind the camera if you please.

JOHN BEAN: Let's go gentlemen.

GAFFER: Script, script, who's got a script? Bernie, what's this say . . . Bernie . . . here . . .

SIR FLUTE: Exterior dawn. Establishing shot. Four soldiers look out over the harbor.

JOHN BEAN: Joe, do I have final cut?

JOE VERIATO: No, John . . . The Film Institute of the United Kingdom of England has final cut . . . they pulled our chestnuts from the fire.

A wail of frustration from JOHN BEAN.

GAFFER: Quiet . . . stand by . . . TURN OVER!

SOUND MAN: Running.

FOCUS PULLER: Speed.

OPERATOR: Mark it.

CLAPPER: Bunker Hill Sequence. Scene One, take one . . .

The CLAPPER *held above his head and very close to* SIR FLUTE.

JOHN BEAN: Action!

The GRIPS *go to the ramparts of earth and jeer at the approaching* BRITISH ARMY. *One of them beats a drum.*
A SPECIAL EFFECTS MAN *pins a french letter filled with imitation blood to the chest of* SIR FLUTE *and then trails from it a wire to his board under the redoubt, where he sits and waits.*
SIR FLUTE *follows the wire in fascination, then he goes cross-eyed as another* SPECIAL EFFECTS MAN *sticks a dab of plasticine to his forehead, follows it up to where another* SPECIAL EFFECTS MAN *squats on a step ladder, a wire from the plasticine in his hand, and held high.*
Enter JOHN BEAN *on the crane. He swoops low over the redoubt and yells:*

JOHN BEAN: FX. Gimme six squibs . . . here, here, here, here, here and Here! You, you, you, and you DIE!

Three of the GRIPS *do, one reluctantly, and after a while he decides to sit up and light a fag.*
THE SPECIAL EFFECTS MAN *in his hole under the redoubt obliges with six puffs of earth across the redoubt in the place indicated by* JOHN BEAN.

JOHN BEAN: CUT! Print it . . . next set up!

Exit JOHN BEAN *on crane.*
Noise of approaching BRITISH ARMY *through all this, drum and fife.*
Re-enter JOHN BEAN *and Crew.*

GAFFER: What's next, guv, sir?

JOHN BEAN: The surrender.

SIR FLUTE: What surrender?

JOHN BEAN: I surrender! Dress some dude in a cloak and have him surrender, get some other guy to give a sword . . .

GAFFER: Maurice, sword, hat, cloak . . .

MAURICE: Props, sword . . .

JOHN BEAN: Joe Veriato?

MAURICE: Mr Veriato?

JOHN BEAN: Joe, I'm gonna make you a movie star.

GAFFER: Call Mr Veriato . . .

JOE VERIATO: I'm here, I'm here . . .

JOHN BEAN: Now, Joe, props sword . . . Joe, cloak and hat . . . now when I tell you to, you take the sword from this guy out of shot, right?
Joe, the shades, give your shades to the . . .
Stand there.

JOE VERIATO: But John, but John . . . but John . . .

JOHN BEAN: No Joe, just stand there on your mark.

GAFFER: Mark!

A GRIP *rushes forward and nails a batten to* JOE's *toes almost, his mark.*

JOHN BEAN: Stand still Joe. Now Joe all you have to do is listen to what I tell you and you will be great just great kid . . . wow!

GAFFER: There's your mark sir, it won't bite you.
Now then, absolute quiet please . . .

GAFFER *takes the sword, holds it. Asks:*

Claw my love, am I out of frame?

OPERATOR: You're clear, Chas . . .

GAFFER: Right, stand by . . . OK Camel? Maurice? Claw? Bernie your volts? Right, stand by . . . Turn OVER!

JOHN BEAN: Action!
No, Joe . . .

GAFFER: Hold the roll . . .

MAURICE: Cut it . . .

JOHN BEAN: Just take the fucking sword . . . Joe. It's the sword of surrender Joe . . . this is a moment of fucking awe Joe . . . you have just won the battle Joe . . . now try again . . .

GAFFER: Standby . . . absolute . . . turn OVER!

JOHN BEAN: Action!
Joe, you are not after a fucking Oscar . . .

GAFFER: Hold the roll!

JOHN BEAN: Now Joe, just do what I tell you Joe, listen and do what I tell you . . . let's try this shot again gentlemen.

GAFFER: Stand by, turnover!

JOHN BEAN: And ACTION! That's it Joe, just take it slowly . . . lots of awe . . . that's it . . . now look at it . . .
fine fine . . . now return it . . .
Great, CUT!
Print it, that was great Joe . . . NEXT!
I want a flag and a guy for the 'Tyranny' speech . . . Flutey, over by the flag, it's a close shot gentlemen, gimme the flag top left of frame . . . Sound, it's a guide track but I want music over . . .

GAFFER: Bernie, give us your brutes, you've got enough of 'em . . . right.

JOHN BEAN: Now Flutey . . . just do as I say, you just stand there . . . I will say the lines for the guide track . . . you just follow my hand . . . right . . .

GAFFER: Right Red Lead . . . stand by with your wind, and a line on Sister Anna's banner . . . right, your gate perfect, Claw?

OPERATOR: Okay.

GAFFER: And absolute fucking quiet if you please. Stand by!

With SIR FLUTE PARSONS *standing by the flag, the wind machine making it flutter and* SOUND *giving us suitable mood music,* JOHN BEAN *directs his actor through.*

JOHN BEAN: Action, close, very close, flag edge of frame, let me see it,
let me see it there, look up at me
Washington, look up, let me see your eyes, set your shoulders square, stand square, let's see some pride, some wisdom in those eyes . . . come on you're the first goddam President of the United States, come on, look up to me . . . you can hear music, dialogue:
"There is something wonderful in what we do, and it isn't common. Oh,
I guess people have fought against
Tyranny before when it got just so rotten there wasn't much else they could do, we English have never been slow
to let Tyrants know just what we think of them . . . but, never before I suggest and I could be wrong but I don't think
I am, never before have those of us who now stand against their might of
Britain
had such simple and strong aims in mind,
simple and strong . . ."
Pause, pause, think about it, okay kid,
now let's hear it, look up, look up,
climb up alongside of that flag.
"We want to be free to build our own country. We want our children to grow strong and lovely in free meadows,
good grass,
sweet water,
decent towns, broad clean streets where a man can meet and talk to his God as a wise neighbour, respect him; maybe a little frightened of him, but welcome

in his fields, his granary, his house.
Where there is no person put over us
who is not KNOWN TO US!
ready to bandy words with us on all manner
of things we've got a right to
talk about,
set down, have a good jaw about
whenever and wherever we all see
fit, on all manner of subjects which
pertain to the common good . . . as
equals, maybe not so clever as the
next man, maybe sometimes a mite
lazy, but each and every one of us a
free man living in a free country,
where we own our land and our lives
because we own our country, signed,
sealed, witnessed and long since
paid for, where the mortgage is only
our damned stubborn willingness to
get up and defend it!"
Wait a minute, wait a minute, pause
a beat, and another, then very close,
strong and quiet and let's see just
a little sadness because you know people
are gonna get killed, kid . . .
"The sword is now drawn and God knows
when it will be sheathed"
CUT! Print the whole goddam thing,
I don't give a shit for the light.

Exit JOHN BEAN *down hill.*

GAFFER: I want a zip up, twenty feet high, here . . .

GRIPS *rush from the redoubt to erect the tower, scaffolding and timber, the bang and crash of battle building. From the tower they build a ramp, from the ramp another ramp, from the ramp another tower. The* GAFFER *directing.*
The whole stage being criss-crossed with construction. Smoke being puffed out by two SPECIAL EFFECTS MEN.
Then, sudden silence.
The sound of drum and fife heard far away down the hill.
Enter an ACTOR *who has run amok. He is dressed in blue military coat, and a blue three-cornered hat.*

ACTOR: I am Colonel Prescott . . . you can't do anything without me . . . I wasn't called . . . who are you?

To SIR FLUTE *standing very still.*

SIR FLUTE: Me?

ACTOR: Yes, you . . . should I be with you? Who are you supposed to be?

SIR FLUTE: I'm supposed to be George Washington . . .

ACTOR: You shouldn't be here, you're miles away at this time . . .

SIR FLUTE: Aaaaah . . . a reader, I hope you haven't read too much, you're going to hate it.
Always a mistake, but they will do it, the intelligent ones . . . the ones can read.

Enter JOHN BEAN *as a bang of cannon erupts.*

JOHN BEAN: More blood . . . more blood, better blood . . . make up . . . that's the wrong colour blood . . . people were starving . . .

He points at a writhing GRIP. *A* MAKE-UP ASSISTANT *rushes onto the stage to spray the* GRIP *with blood.*
Exit JOHN BEAN *on his crane.*
Shouts from the redoubt. ACTOR *rushes forward and says:*

ACTOR: Fire!

SIR FLUTE: Are you Colonel Prescott?

ACTOR: I am, sir.

SIR FLUTE: Then you're on the wrong hill.

ACTOR: I beg your pardon?

SIR FLUTE: Yes, Breed's Hill, that's where you should be, they're not shooting Breed's Hill today, but you've got a lovely scene when the guns come up and you find they haven't made any holes for you to poke them through, marvellous, you say, 'Shoot the damn things straight through the wall, that'll give us holes', marvellous scene . . .

ACTOR: I didn't say that.

SIR FLUTE: Well, no, because we're not shooting it until tomorrow . . .

ACTOR: I am Colonel Prescott, I didn't say that . . .

SIR FLUTE: Aaaaah, books . . . aaaah, well no you didn't but don't you think you should . . . isn't it better you should say it?
I know somebody else said it, but

dramatic licence, you are a highly paid feature artist . . . why not?

ACTOR: I don't feel right saying it when I know that I didn't . . .

SIR FLUTE: I see, but you're still on the wrong hill.

ACTOR: I see.
Will I be noticed, it's my first film?

SIR FLUTE: No no . . . stay, stay . . . it's becoming quite exciting . . . wrong, very wrong, but quite exciting . . . look . . .
You see they weren't quite as silly as all that, the British . . .
You see they didn't just just . . . rush up the bloody hill laden down
with silly packs and things,
though they did have silly packs and things, of course they did, every proper army did then, and hair covered in powder, that sort of things, very smart and took ages to do, pipeclay, that sort of thing, they looked so smart
bags of swank as we used to be told,
chin up, bags of swank,
and they weren't being silly really,
nobody could've expected you Americans to turn out to be quite so good at it,
not really . . .
Are you an American man?
Aaaaah, well you must be sick and tired of it all by now, all this bi business,
I know of a little girl who calls it
the 'bisensual', charming isn't it?
I think we are making more of a fuss of it than you are in a way, I can't imagine why . . . it was so transitory,
I mean it really wasn't long before you were settling down, had settled down and were behaving just like the rest
of us . . . you see unlike the Irish and others you can, like us, always see the other fellow's point of view,
like us you know the meaning of compromise, you can promise one thing when you mean another quite happily, they can't you see, they're so stuck in their ways . . .
They are doing it awfully well, oh it makes one proud to be British, look at them coming, never thought I'd see the Irish in this day and age carrying Union Jacks . . . aaaah, that one isn't any more . . . I do hope he isn't using real bullets, there was a rumour that he might . . .

Enter JOHN BEAN *on crane, shouting:*

JOHN BEAN: More blood!

Exit JOHN BEAN *on crane.*

SIR FLUTE: He's awfully fussy about the colour, they always are . . . I think it needs more blue in it, don't you?

He asks of the ACTOR *who suddenly waves his sword and vanishes in a tumble of earth and timber.*
SIR FLUTE *looks down, says:*

Well done, I'd come with you but I'm wired up you see . . .

The hammering and the drumming and the banging and the explosions start again, as GRIPS *man the redoubt, shoot down on the advancing* BRITISH ARMY, *volley after volley.* SPECIAL EFFECTS MEN, *their faces blackened by powder, crawl and run from charge to charge, hunched running from cannons and powder kegs.*

Now and again there is silence so that the bedlam of noise of another kind can be heard, the voices of people talking, talking, yelling, screaming one to the other, one on top of the other, the voices of MAJOR GENERAL WILLIAM HOWE, HUMPHREY BOGART, LAURENCE OLIVIER, JOE VERIATO, JAMES CAGNEY, SPENCER TRACY, GENERAL ISRAEL PUTNAM, COL. WILLIAM PRESCOTT, GEORGE WASHINGTON, RONALD REAGAN, STEWART GRANGER, EDWARD G. ROBINSON, JOHN WAYNE, RAYMOND MASSEY, CAPTAIN JOHN FORD, JOE VERIATO, LT. COL. ABERCROMBY, SOLDIERS OF THE FIFTH OF FOOT, SOLDIERS OF THE FOURTH OF FOOT, OF THE FIFTY SECOND OF FOOT, MAJOR MONCRIEF, ROBERT RYAN, BETTE DAVIS, HENRY FONDA, JAMES CAGNEY, HUMPHREY BOGART, LAURENCE OLIVIER, CHARLES LAUGHTON, GEORGE ARLISS, SIDNEY GREENSTREET, CAROLE LOMBARD, GEORGE RAFT, GEORGE SANDERS, RAYMOND

MASSEY, MAJOR GENERAL HENRY CLINTON, WARD BOND, CEDRIC HARDWICKE, LIONEL BARRYMORE, DAVID NIVEN, JOE VERIATO, GAFFER, SIR FLUTE PARSONS, DOUGLAS FAIRBANKS, RONALD COLMAN, GARY COOPER, JAMES CAGNEY, HUMPHREY BOGART, LAUREN BACALL, PAULETTE GODDARD, HUMPHREY BOGART AND PHYLLIS CALVERT, LAURENCE OLIVIER AND MAXINE COOPER, JAMES CAGNEY AND DAVID NIVEN, JOE VERIATO AND BETTE DAVIS, . . . AND FREDRIC MARCH AND GEORGE ARLISS AND JOHN GIELGUD AND BRIAN DONLEVY AND DRUMMER ROBERT STEELE, CAPTAIN JOHN CHESTER AND PAUL MUNI AND PETER LORRE AND COLONEL MOSES PARKER.

'Attack all along the goddam line
bum stir crazy stool pigeon this day
you're crazy slip out of Boston hold
fast stand fast run faster than that
the first to run will die will feel
more than the prick of my sword the
flat of my sword what kind of a cheap
crook do you think I am?
some kind of order here some kind of
honour here hanged like a dog
here here you guys man this goddam
fence they're flanking us hold hold
hold this guv will you prayers bury
him without prayers we had better go
forward gentlemen with the news the
money don't move or I'll fill you
full of lead what do you do here you
cur this day you don't have the guts
to use it aim for the groin aim for
their waistbelts aim for his crotch
his yellow belly tarnation I ain't
but got my eye in and they fixin to
run all the way back to Boston to
Los Angeles to Frisco to L.A. to Mexico
we can be across the border tonight
baby just relax just one kiss just get
out sir I cannot love you while my
country is at war while my man is dying
out there while he's rotting in some
crummy jail on some gallows tree in some
lousy jail in some prison hulk
languishing on some bloody field
I shall take command here for your
country's sake honour duty to King
and Country Home Nation Family Of
Man God Truth Reason Life Liberty
one colonel is as good as another
we're all colonels here

Through this the stage has turned to show the BRITISH ARMY *making their repeated attempts on the redoubt and going down like flies.*
Through this JOHN BEAN *has swooped in and out on his crane with his* CREW *yelling above the bedlam, calling the shots:*

JOHN BEAN: I call the shots.
Allowed the wildest escapades the utmost freedom
and I am clothed in luxury with servants and
soldiers at my command my caperings watched with
fascination and envy and awe
given freedom beyond the dreams
beyond the dreams
to destroy and cheat and inspire
create shadows of substance
fill the air with twitterings
I call the shots!
CUT colour going down close
CUT to guns
CUT to Lord Howe "Hang any two . . . You and You
CUT to 52nd of foot
CUT to 4th of foot
CUT to American with blue eyes "Holy Moses they're still coming"
CUT to British Officer, young man with blue eyes
"Reform dam you reform"
Flashback Interior Boston night
Mrs Loring and Lore Howe medium 2 shot
Howe "I love you"
CUT to close up, Mrs Loring
"I love you, kiss me hold me you make me feel so
alive and I give not a fig for convention"
"Your buttons are hurting me, slip into something more comfortable."
"You have the most beautiful lips Mrs
Loring, may I
embrace you on behalf of His Majesty."
"Certainly sir . . . My love your sword is hurting me"
WHIP PAN
CUT to redoubt exterior day
Bunker hill, a roar of cannon

A volly of shot
Smoke, special F.X.
More smoke
CUT to young British Officer his young blue eyes fade
CUT to American Officer his young blue eyes shine
CUT to British army its P.O.V.
They die in lines in powdered, wigged, dressed off lines
Twisting, writhing bodies
CRAB DOLLY . . . CRAB DOLLY . . .
Iris in Mrs Loring, she gives a sigh
Why, she asks, why must so many young men die
CUT to Howe, shouting at his men
CUT to Abercromby close
He drops his head in shame
CUT to Amos Parker drawing a bead on Abercromby
CLAW MOTION . . . SLOW MOTION
CUT to Abercromby, his P.O.V.
CUT to fleeing British
CUT to cheering Americans
CUT to Introspective Howe
Iris in Mrs Loring
"Why did I not treat her as a human being
this woman so full of beauty and charm, why
I call the shots
CUT to Abercromby . . . his P.O.V.
CUT to Levelled musket
CUT to Amos Parker "Theres a lobsterback goddam officer
see here while I shoot His redcoat eyes out
CUT out to Abercromby who faces death
CUT to Putnamleaping sword
"Strike up your gun sir for God's sake spare
that lilly livered redcoat I love him like a brother"
CUT to Abercromby who raises his hat in gratitude
Wrong hat
Dissolve fade . . . Interior Barn Day
"What in Gods name do you do sir"
"Come on baby lets have a little fun here
Stab me but you're a fiery wench
Just one kiss and I'll see that you get to London
meet the king, huh, know what I mean."
CUT to lips . . . Wrong lips . . .
Open the mouth a little honey . . . Make Up
"Just one kiss, he need never know"
"Get out sir, I cannot" . . . Relax . . . eyes flash
Hazel eyes wrong eyes Make Up "Open your legs"
CUT to legs . . . Wrong legs
"I cannot love you while my husband rots in one
of your gaols
"Sure you can honey,
It's only a movie, for Christ's sake
It's only a movie we're making here,
I call the shots
WRAP . . . WIPE . . . DOLLY

JOE VERIATO: I suggested that scene

THROUGH THIS on a screen at the back we are watching a piece of film of a dying MAN *who lies held by his friends on the redoubt, the post sync lines cross and cross and he says something which we don't hear. The dying man* DOCTOR WARREN. *A bevy of ragged buckskin clad, shirt and breeches clad, homespun clad* PATRIOTS *kneel at his side. As the death of Wolfe at Quebec.*

AND THROUGH THIS make-up ASSISTANTS *have been liberal with their blood bottles,* GRIPS *have fought off the advancing forces of reason led by* WESLEY *and* SY HOELMERSBAGGER, *and shoved and hammered white reflectors into position for every shot called by* JOHN BEAN, *the stage has moved through full circle so that the other side of the hill might be seen, trees with bodies of deserters dangling from them, lines of bodies on the hill red and white,* SIR FLUTE *as the pivot to it all.*

Enter WESLEY *and* SY HOELMERSBAGGER *at the head of the* BRITISH ARMY.
Enter MARY JANE PENDEJO *dressed as General Sir Banestre Tarleton in the Joshua Reynolds portrait of him as a young cavalry officer wearing the green uniform and helmet of the British Legion. She shoves at her chest and complains in a high whining voice:*

MARY JANE PENDEJO: Hey John, has anyone seen John? Hey John I just can't keep my tits in this tunic . . .

Noise. Drum and fife. Rattle of musket fire and the GRIPS *are galvanised into activity again and attack the*

BRITISH ARMY.
JOHN BEAN *on foot, excited, calls to the camera, holding his fingers in the classic wide-screen viewing manner:*

JOHN BEAN: Hey, hey you guys gimme a piece of the shit here . . .
Bayonets, I want bayonets . . .

He spins round and an EXTRA *gives him a bayonet where he would least want it. Holds it there for a moment and then* JOHN BEAN *looks at it in his body, astonished. The* EXTRA *pulls it out, horrified.*
GRIPS *rush white screens and it is seen that all the construction has been for this moment as* JOHN BEAN *slumps, looks at the blood trickling through his fingers and shouts to the camera which has vanished:*

JOHN BEAN: Keep turning, keep turning . . . come on, keep turning for fuck's sake, I might be dying here . . .

White screens with faces peering over them.
JOHN BEAN *alone, looking at the blood.*

What kind of blood is this, this blood? I want better blood than this . . .

SIR FLUTE: More blue I think . . .

JOHN BEAN: Right, more blue in it . . . keep turning, keep turning, this is spectacular keep turning . . . more blue.

Enter a MAKE-UP ASSISTANT *with a blood bottle to spray* JOHN BEAN *with blood.*
Enter DAN RASHUR *like Fortinbras.*
Enter JOE VERIATO *to hold* JOHN BEAN's *head in exactly the same way as the loop going on and on above their heads.*

JOE VERIATO: John, I want you to know that you have the final cut on this picture.

JOHN BEAN *dies.*

Keep turning.

JOE VERIATO *goes to* DAN RASHUR *and takes him by the hand.*

JOE VERIATO: Dan, he was a great man and he would've wanted you to go on.

MARY JANE PENDEJO: Dan darling, honey, I don't want to complain but I can't keep my bosom in this tunic . . .

SIR FLUTE *still in position asks mildly:*

SIR FLUTE: Do you think I might have my money now?

His chest explodes. The arrow threaded on the wire to his forehead is released by the SPECIAL EFFECTS MAN *and sticks into the plasticine.*

Before there's another accident?

The Curtain comes down.

The post sync loop goes on over the curtain and words are thrown at it, all miss.

THE END

DINGO

Dingo opened at the Bristol Arts Centre on 28 April 1967. It was subsequently presented at the Royal Court Theatre on 15 November 1967, with the following cast:

DINGO	Tom Kempinski
MOGG	Leon Lissek
TANKY	Mark Jones
NAVIGATING OFFICER	John Hussey
COMIC	Henry Woolf
HERO COLONEL/FIRST BLONDE	Eric Allan
COMMANDANT/ROMMEL	Barry Stanton
HERO SCOT/SECOND BLONDE	Robert Booth
HERO DIGGER/THIRD BLONDE	Ian Collier
HERO SIKH/FOURTH BLONDE	Gareth Forwood
HERO AND WILLIE	Michael Francis
HERO ADC/FIFTH BLONDE	Neville Hughes

Directed by Geoffrey Reeves
Designed by Charles Wood and Bernard Culshaw

Dingo was first performed in this version by the Royal Shakespeare Company at The Other Place, Stratford-upon-Avon, on 1 June 1976, with the following cast:

DINGO	Paul Shelley
MOGG	Paul Moriarty
TANKY	Richard Griffiths
NAVIGATING OFFICER	John Bown
COMIC	Ian McDiarmid
HERO FROG/FIRST BLONDE (HAROLD)	Tim Brierley
COMMANDANT	Brian Coburn
HERO SCOT/BLONDE/DOCTOR/ADC	Greg Hicks
HERO AUSSIE/WILLIE	Duncan Preston
HERO COLONEL/BLONDE/OFFICER	Keith Taylor
HERO SIKH/BLONDE/OFFICER	Paul Whitworth

Directed by Barry Kyle
Designed by Kit Surrey

It was subsequently presented at the Warehouse theatre on 26 January 1978, with the following cast changes:

HERO AUSSIE/WILLIE	Alfred Molina
FIRST BLONDE (HAROLD)	Allan Hendrick

GLOSSARY: GENTIAN VIOLET – Medication for Desert Sores; BENZINA – Petrol; STARLIGHT – Royal Army Medical Corps; EYETIE – Italian; BREW-UP – Tea-break or a tank on fire; GONE FOR A SHIT WITH A RUG WRAPPED ROUND HIM – Missing or dead; MYLEASH IT – Forget it; BONDHOOK – Rifle; SWADDIE – Soldier; WADI – Sand Depression; GONE UP TO ANNIE'S ROOM – Gone absent; GARI – A Cart; RONSON – Tank (from their tendency to catch fire); ACKERS – Money; KLIM TIN – Milk Tin; DIENST – An escape.

ACT ONE

Scene One

A sangar made of stones. MOGG *and* DINGO *are dressed in khaki gone yellow trousers/ shorts with webbing equipment, battle order, faded almost white, and boots scuffed white, hair bleached white. Legs, where you can see them through tatters and between short skirt of* MOGG's *shorts and his hose tops/puttees, are deep black brown, red, splashed with gentian violet. Faces are burned, bloated, splashed with gentian violet. Arms likewise. They lie prone and look over the sangar.*

MOGG: You've got a bloated face and your limbs are bloated up.

DINGO: And you Jack.

MOGG: So have I.

DINGO: Gentian violet.

MOGG: I think it attracts the flies.

DINGO: Like cake.

MOGG: Don't make me laugh.

DINGO: I shall shortly piss gentian violet.

MOGG: Then piss some over me.

DINGO: The thing about fighting a desert war . . .

MOGG: We agreed not to talk about it.

DINGO: I must state it for them.

MOGG: Piss some over me because my sores are lifting up their flaming lips.

DINGO: The thing about fighting in the desert is that it is a clean war – without brutality. And clean limbed – without dishonourable actions on either side.

MOGG: They say.

DINGO: And there are no civilians.

MOGG: Except me – I'm a civilian.

DINGO: What am I then?

MOGG: Try as I may – I can't see you standing for a number eight bus picking your nose with the edge of your paper.

DINGO: Or barbarity.

MOGG: I've never stopped being a civilian.

DINGO: Or frightfulness.

MOGG: No refinements.

DINGO: I think you are a civilian.

MOGG: I can't deny that – I find the climate most exhilarating . . .

DINGO: Characteristic of a civilian.

MOGG: You'll find the climate most exhilarating.

DINGO: Take for instance the shit beetle – a more exhilarative sight . . .

MOGG: And I find excitement bubbling within me . . .

DINGO: . . . you never shat.

MOGG: . . . at the nearness of the enemy.

DINGO: Characteristic of a civilian.

MOGG: Or a soldier.

DINGO: When did we last brew up?

MOGG: The inevitable brew up.

DINGO: Thumbs up.

MOGG: Desert fashion – the old brew up.

DINGO: You take the old benzina.

MOGG: Take the old sand.

DINGO: Take the old brew can.

MOGG: Sand.

DINGO: Benzina.

MOGG: And you take the old dixie.

DINGO: Water.

MOGG: In the old dixie.

DINGO: Benzina.

MOGG: On the old sand.

DINGO: Light the old benzina.

A flash, and they have gone, into their hole.

Scene Two

A sangar made of stones. A tank burns. Smoke from a burning tank oils black across the sky. A TANKMAN *with goggles and white face, where the goggles have kept his face clean of caking dust and protected from the sun, skids into the hole with* MOGG *and* DINGO. *He is burning too – but he beats out the flames. Screams from the burning tank shrill through the low thudding battle noise. Inside the tank* CHALKY WHITE *burns to death and screams. They hardly notice him.*

TANKY: I burned my hands.

DINGO: Your lot's over there.

TANKY: Oh yes?

DINGO: Back there – two hundred yards.

MOGG: I should go and report to three and fourpence.

DINGO: I shouldn't hang on here – you can do no good here.

TANKY: It's Chalky.

DINGO: It is?

MOGG: I should tell them that.

TANKY: He's in there.

DINGO: Yes – he is isn't he?

TANKY: Look – I tried to open his hatch. He couldn't open his hatch you see – it was glowing red hot all round his hatch – can you imagine his skin against that?

MOGG: I put my hand on a stove once.

DINGO: Silly bleeder.

TANKY: I burned my hands.

MOGG: I took all my hand off.

DINGO: What a stupid fartarsing thing to do.

TANKY: Pulling.

DINGO: Couldn't you put a bullet in him?

TANKY: I couldn't do that – he's a good lad.

MOGG: That's how I felt – I felt like chopping it off . . . I felt as if the whole of my hand was flaming up – you know what I mean? I saw it flaming in bed for weeks after . . .

TANKY: Shut up Chalky – belt up you bastard.

DINGO: That's it. Get it out of your system – you'll feel better.

MOGG: Burn – you bastard.

TANKY: I've got to get him out.

DINGO: He owe you money?

MOGG: He'll be all right when his brain goes.

TANKY: He'd do it for me.

MOGG: Maybe it's gone already.

TANKY: That's it – he'll not feel anything will he?

DINGO: Roll on death.

TANKY: It's a clean way to go though isn't it?

MOGG: The wogs prefer it.

DINGO: They'd do their nuts if you offered to bury them tidy.

MOGG: They prefer it.

DINGO: He must have been a tough bloke.

MOGG: They're all toughies in the Lancers – aren't they boy?

DINGO: I admire it.

MOGG: I wish I could be the same.

TANKY: I ought to try to get him out.

DINGO: I should go and tell your C.O.

MOGG *rises to* TANKY *above the sangar.*

MOGG: Two hundred yards due south – turn left at the Rifleman's grave and right again where you see the flies . . .

DINGO: Don't poke about – it'll only depress you.

MOGG: We all come to it. (*Sits at right end of sangar again.*)

DINGO: That's where you'll find him – with any luck you'll catch Starlight* too . . .

TANKY: I can't listen – I can't listen.

*Army code for R.A.M.C.

MOGG: He wouldn't want you to.

DINGO: He'd want you to go on.

TANKY: Can't you do something – shoot him – blow it up – shoot him?

CHALKY *stops screaming.*

DINGO: There.

MOGG: That's better for you.

TANKY: I tried to pull him out didn't I?

MOGG: Back there – figures two hundred or so back there turn left at the Rifleman . . .

They put on steel helmets with red bands and grab TANKY *by either arm.*

TANKY: He brewed up didn't he?

DINGO: Right – move on trooper – rejoin your unit.

MOGG: . . . and right again where you see the flies.

DINGO: Battle police.

MOGG: Rejoin your unit.

TANKY: Battle police . . . ?

DINGO: Royal Corps of . . .

MOGG: You'll find your R.H.Q. due south . . .

TANKY: Thanks.

DINGO: Our job.

MOGG: We know where everyone is.

DINGO: Any time.

MOGG: We got you up here.

DINGO: Yes – if it wasn't for us Jack you'd still be swanning about the desert looking for a battle.

MOGG: Due south.

TANKY: Thanks.

DINGO: Remember me to the Colonel.

TANKY: If you see Chalky . . .

MOGG: We'll bury him.

DINGO: Only we won't see him – we don't get any action.

Another scream starts.

TANKY: That's him again.

MOGG: We promise you it's not.

DINGO: You can take it from us mate – that's foreign.

TANKY: I can't bear it.

MOGG: No. It's not Chalky.

DINGO: He thinks it's Chalky.

MOGG: Look – it's foreign. No British squaddie goes on like that.

DINGO: Go out and finish him if you like.

TANKY: No – let the bastard scream.

MOGG: He'll belt up shortly (*He does.*) There – these fucking Eyeties haven't got the stamina.

TANKY: Funny that.

DINGO: It wasn't.

TANKY: I don't know how you do it.

MOGG: Due south two hundred yards . . .

They release him and shoo him off up right.

TANKY: It's Chalky.

DINGO: You tell them . . .

TANKY: . . . get him on the blood wagon – quack'll fix him up won't he? Left at the Rifleman's grave?

MOGG: . . . right again at the flies . . .

DINGO: Don't mess about with the flies . . .

TANKY *goes – bent double and running.*

MOGG: . . . straight up the minefield.

DINGO: It's a clean way to go.

They take off their helmets.

MOGG: How do you know the difference?

DINGO: What – between the screams?

MOGG: Yes – you can't tell one from the other. You were taking the piss.

DINGO: No.

MOGG: They all sound the same to me mate.

DINGO: No.

MOGG: Go on.

DINGO: Tell you what – next one . . . half a sheet – right?

MOGG: You're on.

DINGO: Eyes down.

They duck flat behind the sangar wall.

Scene Three

A Desert Battle. A NAVIGATING OFFICER *on a bicycle navigates his battalion in front of nobody – his eyes tight on the compass he's holding. He waves nobody on . . . Nobody follows him. He stops – takes a bearing with commendable courage and waves again to nobody behind him.* DINGO *peeks over the top.*

DINGO: Half a sheet the next one to scream is clean, dry and slightly upper class white English.

MOGG: You can't tell all that.

DINGO: Half a sheet.

MOGG: That was him then – going across.

DINGO: But I don't know do I? I don't know as whether he'll scream.

MOGG: You can be dead certain can't you?

DINGO: How can I? There's a lot of luck.

MOGG: Bloody twister. If you've seen him.

DINGO: Scrub it.

MOGG: No – I'll let it stand.

DINGO: Scrub it.

MOGG: No – but it's nigh on a dead cert. If you've seen him. Gone for a shit with the rug wrapped round him.

DINGO: I said scrub it – scrub it.

MOGG: You only guess anyway.

DINGO: I know.

MOGG: Down.

They down. The NAVIGATING OFFICER *navigates his way to their hole and stops.*

NAVIGATING OFFICER: This is Green (*He kneels between them.*)

DINGO: No.

MOGG: You mean this is Blue.

NAVIGATING OFFICER: No – this is Green.

MOGG: Blue.

MOGG *and* DINGO *pretend to don headsets and use a radio.*

DINGO: Hello Two One Able – we are at Blue – Two One Able Over.

MOGG: Hello Two One Able – say again – Over.

NAVIGATING OFFICER: Green.

DINGO: Hello Two One Able – I say again – we are at Blue – Two One Able Over.

NAVIGATING OFFICER: No.

MOGG: Two One Able – Roger – How far from Green – Over.

DINGO: Two One Able – figures fower miles – Over.

MOGG: Two One Able – Roger – Out.

NAVIGATING OFFICER: You're wrong.

DINGO: Blue.

MOGG: Blue.

NAVIGATING OFFICER: Green.

DINGO: Blue.

MOGG: Blue.

NAVIGATING OFFICER (*courageously*): Green.

DINGO: Listen – Blue.

MOGG: All right Jack? Blue.

NAVIGATING OFFICER: I know Green – when I see it.

DINGO: Blue.

MOGG: Blue.

DINGO: We know blue when we see it.

NAVIGATING OFFICER *studies his map – worried.*

MOGG: Hello Two One Able – Position – Two One Able Over.

DINGO: Hello Two One Able – Position – Wait . . . Wait Out.

MOGG: Blue.

NAVIGATING OFFICER: Ask them if they know where Green is.

DINGO: Hello Two One Able – Position – Blue – I say again Blue . . . where is Green? Two One Able – Over.

MOGG: Two One Able – Left at the Rifleman's grave – Over.

DINGO: Two One Able – Roger – Out.

They leap to attention.

MOGG: Sir.

NAVIGATING OFFICER: I know. Left at the Rifleman's grave. I know – I'm a navigating officer. (*Stands between them.*)

DINGO: Then you would know wouldn't you sir.

MOGG: The thing is sir – we're not sure . . .

DINGO: Sappers sir – we was asked to move to blue and set up a water point sir.

MOGG: . . . We're not sure we should start pumping or not sir . . .

DINGO: Point is – the whole army'll be looking for blue . . .

NAVIGATING OFFICER: This is Blue.

DINGO: Sir.

MOGG: Then we should set up our water point here sir?

NAVIGATING OFFICER: Set up your water point here. At Blue.

DINGO: Sir.

NAVIGATING OFFICER: I am moving to Green.

MOGG: Due south two hundred yards – left . . .

NAVIGATING OFFICER: . . . I know – at the Rifleman's grave – I'm a navigating officer. (*Pedals off muttering as he looks at his map.*)

DINGO: Right again at the flies.

The NAVIGATING OFFICER *goes.*

Eyes on compass and very daring upright posture.

MOGG: Straight up the minefield.

They relax and wait for the bang . . . Nothing.

DINGO: I was wrong.

MOGG: About the next one.

DINGO: It was a mistake anyone could make.

MOGG: Half a sheet.

They wander downstage preparing to sit in their old positions.

DINGO: Men's lives.

MOGG: What of it?

DINGO: Don't you find it ghoulish betting money on men's lives?

MOGG: Myleash it then.

DINGO: Typical civilian. It's like half a sheet on whether Jesus . . . isn't it?

MOGG: Declare it null.

DINGO: No. No – I'll pay up. I want to pay up. I want to see the disgusting ghoulish way your tongue comes out to look at the money.

MOGG: I don't bet on men's lives. I bet on their screams.

DINGO: Torturer.

MOGG: It's only whether or not – that's all. It's not pressing the tit . . . pulling the pin, trigger, bayonet out. Anyway Jesus was a foregone conclusion . . . I wouldn't have had anything on him.

DINGO: Here. (*Tosses ten shillings on the floor.*)

MOGG: I don't want it.

DINGO: Pick it up off the floor.

MOGG *begins to bend.*

MOGG: Bend down?

DINGO: Pick it up. (*Sits on the sangar.*)

MOGG: I'm sick and bloody tired of you. I want to get back to being frightened. I want to get back to the lads and run slack-arsed through the dust pointing my bondhook* for ripping. I haven't had a good toss off in months. I'm full up to here with dirty water sit and scratch my navel. I want to stick it in and think it's gone. I've got nothing to inspire me.

DINGO: You don't.

MOGG: No – I don't. But I want you to know that I'm not satisfied with the life we're leading.

DINGO: Do you think I am?

MOGG: It's different for you – in it? (*Sits by* DINGO.)

DINGO: You're starting.

MOGG: Well – it is.

DINGO: How's it different for me then?

MOGG: Well I'm differently placed aren't I? It's a well-known fact it's different for regular swaddies.

DINGO: How's it a well-known fact.

MOGG: Due to it being your trade in it? You're a soldier by trade en't you. You don't find it like we do – like having it off do you? I find it exhilarating . . .

DINGO: You're a fucking farceur.

MOGG: Get in Joseph – it's your birthday. (*Brandishes his bayonet.*)

DINGO: Make tracks then. Only don't come back to me all minus and ask me to bandage you up . . . don't come back to me all red at the seams and ask me to push it back. You think I don't get these feelings? Don't think I don't get these feelings, Mogg. I'm just as randy as you are, Mogg. I have a good brisk run round the battlefield and make do with my mirage.

MOGG: She gets on my tits. (*Picks up his Men Only.*)

DINGO: Shouldn't you be getting on hers?

MOGG: I'm sick and tired of my bleeding mirage.

DINGO: You should have thought of that. You should think of a better one then – shouldn't you?

*Rifle.

MOGG: You can't be blamed for your mirage.

DINGO: I can blame you.

MOGG: How can you? It's an act of God in it?

DINGO: Don't bring him into it – God's a wog – he wants to get back where he came from.

MOGG: See how it goes. We can always come back.

DINGO: I've been dreaming on and off – while the fleas leave go my bollocks on and off. I had a dream last night/ the night before – they're all the same, cold, black – it was the night before.

MOGG: Give it another try. Let's see how it goes.

Dingo *stands at* MOGG's *left.*

DINGO: Shit in it a minute will you? This dream . . . it was me and you standing stark bollock naked as the day we was born holding hands together under the stars . . . No it wasn't. I romanticise. This dream – it was you and me in a wadi, sand that slid under us boots to show like bones out of legs – pieces of blokes . . . and you'd scarpered. I looked all over the shop for you – you'd gone up to Annies room,* you had.

MOGG: I'm proud of you.

DINGO: Mickey – I wouldn't tell a lie. No – I tell a lie . . .

MOGG: We can come back.

DINGO: This dream – one of us. (*Sits on sangar.*)

MOGG: One of us. What about 'one of us'?

DINGO: That's it. Just one of us.

MOGG: What?

DINGO: Which. More like which?

MOGG: Why can't I change my bleeding mirage . . .

DINGO: Why can't you change your bleeding mind?

*Gone absent

MOGG: I can – I've changed my mind – I'm stopping here.

DINGO: I'll believe that when I see your mirage. (*Lies out full length.*)

MOGG: Here. You seen this? They seen yours Dingo?

DINGO: If they were in last night they have – haven't they? I'm satisfied.

MOGG: His mirage is an old bag. here – her teeth. Now then – her teeth so rotten they've marched into open order, separated up. They lean . . . now then, they lean in her stinking mouth, forwards, right and left, front and rear, advance and retire.

DINGO: I'm satisfied. (*Lies face to the hot overhead sun. He has his hands behind his head.*)

MOGG: He's satisfied.

DINGO: Don't mock.

MOGG: His mirage – here have you seen her dugs, swingers, so low they hang on her belt . . . scabby manky old dugs which swing so low they hit her round the earhole when she's washing . . . which she doesn't do, manky old pusher, she stinks up from the neck of her siren suit, she stinks from her gut, she stinks from her yellow teeth . . . the yellow grass on her tongue, hanging from her scabby nostrils . . . his mirage, his mirage is catching . . . Hey, limey, don't kiss that girl, she's just been sucking my snotty cock!

DINGO: It's a question of taste – in it?

MOGG: I'd rot in my lips. My lips would ulcerate – just forced to stand chatting her toe to toe.

DINGO: Depends on what you want. (*Sits up.*) Now then – him. His mirage is all stories. You look and shift in your seat for the heat – I scald my balls . . . I'll grant you that – only it's all stories. His mirage is stories. Her long blonde hair hangs down her back . . . is stories.

MOGG: I'm satisfied.

DINGO: What you ticking for then?

MOGG: I'm not ticking – I'm just not satisfied.

DINGO: Don't say you are then. (*Lies back.*)

MOGG: My mirage is all stories – her long blonde hair is stories. Her big alabaster blue subtle veined breasts is stories – her soft wave of honey milk breath is stories.

DINGO: In soft covers.

MOGG: Scrape your mind for stories in every kind of cover – soft, hard, plain brown not to reveal, silent, and musical . . . They come up coloured. They come up described. They come up blueprint to the last short hair. They don't come up with holes in 'em that's all. You ever tried to stuff a story?

DINGO: Mine's no story. She may be a scrubber – but she's warm and she smells and you touch her . . .

MOGG: Not me – with your's.

DINGO: Mine's real.

MOGG: Mine's a big woman.

DINGO: But she does you no good.

MOGG: Once I thought I'd got it, you know how you do . . . it was a real day for sun on the back of the head and mirages were leaping about like kids on the beach . . . between her legs I found a breech-block . . . did I tell you I was going to be a gunner, I was put in for gunning . . . when I pulled her arm the breech said a small word through the grease . . . it said 'chunk chunk' and opened a chink. Ladies out of uniform 'loaded' you cry and your balled fist is lifted up smooth as silk . . . it started to slide this big girl's breech, and then it stuck . . . I pulled on that arm for ever, my sweat little apples . . . and no more, no more words, no more small words . . . no breech would open.

DINGO: All stories.

MOGG: All smooth.

DINGO: All hard centres.

MOGG: Don't tell me you find joy.

DINGO: Every time.

MOGG: If we go. (*Sits by* DINGO.)

DINGO: If we go – there's still mirages in the afternoon.

MOGG: No – not that . . . If we go – what do you mean one of us – what you said?

DINGO: Christ I sweat.

They look up at the sun.

MOGG: The sun's up.

DINGO: Christ I shiver.

MOGG: Come up sun . . .

DINGO: The ball in my head is red.

MOGG: Come up sun on the small of my back . . .

DINGO: The sun is so scalding it's white. The ball in my head is white and it shimmers from left frontal lobe to right frontal lobe – spit on a stove . . .

Speech is slow from dry mouth and big tongues that fit the bore of the mouth tight as a cartridge case. The wonder is that they talk at all with this cartridge case hot and expanded after firing tight in their black mouth breeches.

MOGG: My time. This time – I'll mirage up a belly dancer – Farouk Farouk bollocks on a hook – belly dancer with navel ten feet and longer deep in the belly stretching here to wherever.

DINGO: I'm still satisfied.

MOGG: Ten feet deep. Fill that in.

DINGO: Ambition.

MOGG: And she do – I'll take up my bondhook and fight.

DINGO: And you do, and you do . . . I had this dream . . . Mickey Mogg one of us.

Music. Not connected music – just wild notes till they come together for a belly dance tune. They dance above the sangar. They lie flat. Arms out flat in the no hard overhead sun, and then they masturbate.

*TANKY *comes in and sits on the sangar.* TANKY *carries* CHALKY. CHALKY *has been burned to death in a sitting position. He is black; charred, thin as a black, dried-in-the-sun, long dead bean. His arms are bent over his pin-head to open his hatch. Bits of still intact khaki drill flap from the crook of his elbows, crutch, and round his ankles. He sits on* TANKY's *knee. While* TANKY *talks to him.*

TANKY: Drunk again. (DINGO *and* MOGG *flip flap hands and groan.)* Chalky's pissed again. Will you rattle should I shake you? Or will you slosh? Remember the leaves all had water on them Chalky my son/my old mucker, clambering back into where was it? You pissed yourself at the water on the laurels . . . water you cried . . . tasted of metal, soot. It was really humorous. And you sat down with me laughing, wet through, pulled by the tab of my jacket down to you, bum in mud . . . in my ear while my booted foot swayed to the laugh of my belly . . . 'to the guard' – 'stand to the guard – I'll wake the bloody guard . . . bring out the guard in the rain – 'stand to the guard by the seaside'. You shouted. You said, 'Stand to the Blackpool Tower guard.' For there are spies up the Blackpool Tower watching us wash the water up from Ireland between our – stinking dirt and sock fluff between the ranks – military toes. You were aggressive. This beer's watered down, this beer's adulterated with pig's piddle. It's all we can get now Jack. Try it on your hair for a tonic. Splash splash – up through the leaves on your face.

DINGO: Ninety-nine, change hands.

MOGG: Don't care if I do go blind.

The sun is not so hot now. DINGO *and* MOGG *sit/stand up. They rub their crutches, DINGO happy,* MOGG *ruefully.*

MOGG: Again!

DINGO: Did you get him in?

*An additional scene from the original version may be incorporated here as Scene Four. Tanky's entrance would then begin Scene Five. See Appendix A.

TANKY: I got him out.

MOGG: That's it . . . (*They notice the proud, grinning* TANKY. *They stand either side of him.*) . . . Now for the other.

DINGO: What you got there?

MOGG: Where did you get that?

DINGO: You.

TANKY: I got him out.

DINGO: You've been picking up things on the battlefield.

TANKY: Chalky.

MOGG: Oh my God – get it dug in.

DINGO: This sun.

MOGG: Brings out the worst – you'll have it very bad if it turns.

DINGO: I'm disgusted. You tramp feet raw looking for a bleeding place where you don't have to cuddle corpses so as you don't have to lose all sense . . . Keep some sense of fitness . . .

MOGG: Arrives on a gari.

DINGO: Get it dug in. (*Bends nearer for emphasis.*) What's the matter with you? You puggled? You're puggled – can't you take simple direct instructions? Don't concern you Jack. Take it somewheres else.

MOGG: Left at the Rifleman's grave . . .

DINGO: He's been there – you been there?

MOGG: He's been there has he? Notice an officer looking for Green?

TANKY: Chalky. I got him out see. I told you I'd get him out – I wouldn't let him down.

DINGO: You ain't been there then have you?

MOGG: A thought just struck me . . .

DINGO: They've had it cleared. Well you're not the only one – that thought struck me. Who do you reckon he is anyway?

MOGG: . . . they could have cleared it – or they could have stepped on them all. That could have happened.

DINGO: Oh yes – what sort of minefield is that then – it might be your idea of a minefield – it's not mine . . . You can't call a minefield a minefield unless it's like currants in a cake – every now and then a bleeding great sultana – that's a minefield. You didn't walk through that.

MOGG: He'd have a bloody crutch if he did.

DINGO: Too true. (*They look at* TANKY, *who smiles.*) And who do you reckon he is?

TANKY: Chalky.

MOGG: That . . . ?

DINGO: Oh yes . . . highly likely. (MOGG *sits by* TANKY.) How do you make that out then? You had a good butchers at it? No – well go on – have a good shuft. Emotions apart – have a good hard shufti at that pipe cleaner you got sitting on your lap.

MOGG: Bears no relation.

DINGO: That?

MOGG: Bears no relation to the British Soldier.

DINGO: None whatever.

MOGG: Just doesn't compare.

TANKY: I couldn't leve him there . . . for all and sundry – I surely couldn't loose him down could I? I had to see you were all right . . .

During this the COMIC *pushes on his booth. It is a mobile theatre with lights and flags and a platform for the* COMIC *to perform on.*

DINGO: Stone me.

MOGG: He's talking to it.

DINGO: Like it was something.

TANKY: . . . didn't I Chalky? Well – he only lives up the road.

COMIC: Leave the first three rows for the officers will you?

COMIC *comes to between* MOGG *and* DINGO. MOGG *is happy – almost excited.* DINGO *is agitated.*

DINGO: What's this George?

COMIC: We entertain you. Stand Easy and let yourself go – it's the Tails up and Lick 'em show. Just keep the first three rows for the officers will you – I thank you.

MOGG: I thank you.

DINGO: Don't laugh – don't encourage him.

MOGG: I like a laugh.

DINGO: I don't mind the occasional lost, stolen, or bleeding strayed half-cock swaddie – I don't mind the odd pig ignorant leading his band of happy heroes . . .

MOGG: Tit show is it?

DINGO: We've seen it George.

MOGG: I ain't seen it.

DINGO: You've seen it. Saw it yesterday.

TANKY *walks* CHALKY *to the right.*

COMIC: What you think of the show then? Mind you I've played Green before – I always go down very well at Green . . .

MOGG: Leg show is it?

COMIC: Brought the house down I did with my 'Man does not live by Bread alone' gag. You like that one . . . it's a lovely story. Always goes down well before a killing match.

MOGG: Tit show is it?

DINGO: You can't play Green again can you?

COMIC: Oh no – mind you it's a nice theatre.

TANKY: Hey – Chalky's pissed again.

Walks CHALKY *in front of him – makes him sway about like a drunk.* COMIC *goes over to him.*

COMIC: A vent – lovely act. Always goes down well.

DINGO: Sorry. We've booked him – ventriloquist.

COMIC: Double booking? No – can't be. Where's this then?

DINGO: Green.

COMIC: Can't be.

DINGO: That's right in it?

NAVIGATING OFFICER *rides on and drops his bike centre. Come to above sangar.*

MOGG: Is it a Tit show?

NAVIGATING OFFICER: This is Blue.

COMIC: There you are – I've played Blue too many times for that – no fly space. Mind you it's an easy show.

TANKY: Chalky likes a good laugh – don't you mate? (*He answers himself as* CHALKY *– a high-pitched pursed lip voice.*)

CHALKY: Too bloody true.

DINGO (*by the* NAVIGATING OFFICER): No sir – this is Green sir.

NAVIGATING OFFICER: Very humorous . . .

COMIC: Very nice sir.

TANKY: No – it's only me really.

COMIC: Very nice.

DINGO: Because we had him last night sir – very good show . . . that 'Man does not live by Bread alone' gag – been pissing ourselves all day over that . . .

COMIC *takes* CHALKY *on his knee.*

COMIC: Can you do the old drink of water business?

The sky darkens. DINGO *stands in the middle of the stage and shouts.*

DINGO: This is Green.

OFFICER: No.

MOGG: He's a navigating officer.

NAVIGATING OFFICER: This is Blue . . .

MOGG: Where they have the tit shows . . .

NAVIGATING OFFICER: Where they have the water point.

DINGO: This is Green – this is Green.

NAVIGATING OFFICER: You want Green?

MOGG: I can help you out there . . . two hundred yards due south – left at the . . .

NAVIGATING OFFICER: Pull pull yourself together.

DINGO: Green.

Takes out his toilet roll; hands the NAVIGATING OFFICER *a piece.*

OFFICER: Have you got a map? Right – got a map? Right – figures two hundred yards due south – left at the Rifleman's grave . . . Do you think your officers – I am an officer you know – I'm a navigating officer, lead on navigating officer, do you think your officers don't know one stretch of desert from another?

DINGO: Green.

OFFICER: Green – I do know where know where Green is you know – we all know where green is – right? Green was won after heavy fighting, and navigating. Green will go down like Longstop and Knightsbridge. I would have preferred it something catchy like silly mid-on or underarm ridge, but mustn't bellyache. Green is etched deep and honourably on the hearts of gallant men who died that there might be a chapter headed Green. Blazoned in letters of gold on their regiment's colour is Green. Green cost dear. Green is two hundred yards due south – turn left at the Rifleman's grave and right again at the flies . . .

MOGG: Don't poke around with the flies.

NAVIGATING OFFICER: Only lower your morale.

MOGG: . . . straight up the minefield. *(Smiles at* DINGO. COMIC *runs up and uncovers his booth, climbs on.)* Bum titty bum titty bum bum bum.

COMIC: It's the Tails Up and Lick 'em show.

The COMIC *stands on his stage and opens the show – music blaaaaarts out of nowhere.* MOGG, TANKY *and the* NAVIGATING OFFICER *sit on the floor in front on the stage.* DINGO *hovers separate.*

DINGO: What sort of minefield is that. Minefield . . .

MOGG/TANKY: Hurrah, Hurrah!

COMIC: That's all right mother – plenty of room in the stalls . . . (DINGO *sits.*) Don't mind me – I'm an idle abortionist – I specialise in struggling actresses who didn't.

TANKY: Didn't what?

COMIC: Struggle. (*The* HEROES *enter over the mound helping the* COLONEL *to a seat.*) At ease, Colonel. He's suffering from bottle fatigue . . . We were married by candle light but she got on my wick . . . (*The stage gets darker and darker until there is only light on the* COMIC's *small stage.* DINGO *doesn't laugh. The* COMIC *puts on a beret with two badges in it.*) My first encounter with Rommel was of great interest – luckily I had time to sort out the mess and the Jock columns and get some sort of willingness from below due to grip from above. I don't smoke and I don't drink but I do grip and I did see him off. No trouble there and the ball's in my court which I won when it was his service . . . now it is my service – the score standing at one-love . . . Talking of love did you hear the one about the gippo bint with the pieyard, as they call their bow-wows. A pissyarse digger jig-a-jigs this sister out of bounds one night – say Sheila what's the dog for? Something new Johnny.

DINGO: Why what you got? Leprosy?

COMIC: Two pounds Johnny, and a pound for the dog, Johnny, what? He licks the back of your neck – just on paradise and bells and green waves lapping the timeless ocean – came the raid . . . redcaps thick on the ground like so much blood . . . the bint gets a belting, a redcap and a dose of clap hands for daddy – the digger gets jankers, a runny nose and a thing about pieyards . . . the dog? He got his licence endorsed. Yap Yap. Thank you, thank you. (*A burst of spandau silences the laughter.*) Welfare . . . Man does not live by bread alone . . . The British Soldier properly led responds to challenge and not to welfare benefits. He will do anything you ask of him so long as he gets his letters, the local rag, and, curiously enough, plenty of tea . . .

TANKY: Can you hear me, mother?

COMIC: He then likes to know, with his tea, what, just what, is going on in the killing ground, and what, just what, you require him to do. He gets anxious if his home town is bombed, smashed squeezed to powder and paint, signal red, and he can't get news about his wife, his girl and his children . . .

A burst of spandau. The COLONEL *leaps to his feet.*

HERO COLONEL: That is too much. First bit of relaxation I've had in months.

HERO SCOT: Is yon bothering you Colonel? Get out the road! (*Slides into the night.*)

HERO COLONEL: Without more ado this gentleman of Scotland – for he was a real gentleman although born in humble and disgusting circumstances and twice convicted of rape with a blunt instrument once convicted of the Gorbals on a Saturday belongs to me . . . belongs to me . . . he slides into the night. Saying 'Is yon bothering ye at all Colonel Harry sir.' He knew I hadn't had a bit of relaxation in weeks. (*Sits down.*)

MOGG: Did you see that?

DINGO: I saw it.

The COMIC *watches the* SCOT HERO *go and sighs with affection – then –*

COMIC: Talking of children. My wife had twins . . . the first time I've been paid twice for the one performance . . . For Chats, Nobby, Winger, and Bummer of K block the Knightsbridge Box from Wren Berker and all the other elastic bottom and tops . . .

They all sing . . . 'We'll meet again' softly, led by the COMIC, *under* DINGO'*s speech.*

DINGO: For my wife who cries, don't cry. Get out and drop your drawers – loosen your blackouts, don't tell me, but let the top of your head go whirl with the stir of Churchill's cigar . . . for my wife who cries – don't cry.

A burst of accordion music.

COMIC: Are you being rude?

Another burst of accordion music – somewhere someone is getting ready to play the accordion. It annoys the HERO COLONEL *who gets to his feet and shouts in exasperation.*

HERO COLONEL: Oh damn. Oh damn it. This is the first bit of relaxation in months.

The doughty HERO DIGGER *strides forward and says:*

HERO DIGGER: Hey cobber, my old sport, digger colonel for a pom . . . is that wop bothering you with his squeezebox? No bight job, you, cobber.

HERO COLONEL: Calls me cobber . . .

HERO DIGGER: Cobber.

HERO COLONEL: Digger.

HERO DIGGER: Cobber. (*Draws bayonet and exits.*)

HERO COLONEL: With that fine contempt for rank, danger, and full of sheer bloody guts and determination that makes him such a fine soldier and endears him to us all . . . calls me . . .

MOGG: Sport.

HERO COLONEL: Sport.

The DIGGER *strides head up into the night.*

MOGG: Sport.

HERO COLONEL: Sport (*Sinks down again.*)

MOGG: Calls me sport.

DINGO (*scorn and anger*): What are you looking for? You, Mogg, I'm talking to you.

COMIC: Man does not live by bread alone. The troops must be brought up to a state of wild enthusiasm before the battle begins . . . Give our gallant Scot a burst of wild enthusiasm.

The HERO SCOT *is back. He sits down.*

DINGO: He willna bother ye any mair, Colonel.

COMIC: I am two hundred per cent fit. I do not believe, no you can't expect troops to win battles unless they are in top-hole condition, top-hole . . .

DINGO: Arsehole.

COMIC: . . . belly-aching will not be tolerated . . . when I first saw belly-aching . . . I am two hundered per cent fit . . . I knew that the commander did not have . . . his finger on the spiritual pulse of his men . . . 'if I do the two-mile run, I will do the two-mile run, sir . . .' He told me, a fat belly-aching Colonel. He stood before me and said . . . 'but if I do the two-mile run sir I will die . . . my doctor says I will die' – he came to me and belly-ached in front of me – no binge 'I will die'. Then I said, I told him . . . 'I would rather you did the two-mile run, colonel, and died now, Colonel, than that you should die later just when we are about to have a battle, it is dashed inconvenient to have officers dying before a battle' . . . he did the run, and as far as I know he did not die. Are you full of binge?

NAVIGATING OFFICER: I'm a navigating officer. I do a deal of running hup hup. (*Leaps up and does high steps round the booth.*)

The accordion is starting into a hymn when it is stopped as if it were strangled. The HERO COLONEL *leaps up.*

COMIC: There there, that. I do not believe troops can succeed unless they are infected with that optimism that comes from well-being.

NAVIGATING OFFICER: Hup hup.

HERO COLONEL: . . . with the light of battle in their eyes and wanting to kill the enemy . . . no commander can inspire or lead even single units without a proper sense of religious truth . . . bottled up in men are great emotional forces . . .

The HERO DIGGER *comes back and tosses the broken accordion at the* HERO COLONEL's *feet.* MOGG *is very impressed. The* HERO COLONEL *is now full of binge. He has lost his fatigue and combs his hair.*

HERO COLONEL: Well done my boy. Be sure that the fine spiritual purpose which inspires us all is clearly expounded to one and all. Men are the raw material with which a commander has to deal . . . he must give them an oulet for the great emotional forces bottled in them, in us all . . . an outlet which is positive and constructive, the thought of which warms the heart and excites the imagination. If you can gain their confidence and their trust, and they feel that their best interests lie in your hands, you have in your possession a priceless asset, and the greatest achievements become possible. (*The* HERO COLONEL *goes to the front of his men. He stands against the low rumbling barrage that is light in the sky. There are many lights in the sky. The* HERO SIKH *goes to fetch him a cup of tea. He gets the mug and walks slowly across the sand so that it shall not be spilled.*) There is a bright gleam that has caught the helmets of our soldiers, it flickers on their bayonets, it laps fiery as brandy in the vessels of their bodies. Eyes jerk and are straightened . . . muscle slides to will of brain. Gone is the evil wasting mist which clogs and clouds so that one's own hand is another man's. Gone is the lifting drunken balloon of tiredness which takes mind aloft to view an empty shell of bloodied khaki filth, your body, your familiar splay of feet, your machinery grinding spit and sand, your sad flutter of hand at thigh . . . (*The music of Elgar floods in.*) Gone. You know you are a man. You know your feet will march on stones that do not shift, you feel your head will watch and command . . . you have peace and you have balance . . . there is once more, there is brightness, for one more time there is steady shining brightness. The light is on our soldiers and they spark in its gleam, for they are steel. They are together welded to a steel!

All this and Elgar too. The HERO SIKH *is blown to bits, just as he reaches the* COLONEL, *and the* COLONEL *blown to the ground; he gets up and dust himself and says:*

HERO COLONEL: Fetch me another mug of tea, someone.

COMIC: I was in the last one. (*He says, cowering in terror.*)

Most of the light comes from the gun-flashes now and the barrage noise grows.

MOGG (*from the hole he has dug for himself*): That's it. You coming? See that? You coming? Fetch me another mug of tea . . . (*Gathers his gear and joins* HEROES.)

DINGO: You're a bleeding hero, Mickey Mogg.

NAVIGATING OFFICER: I'm a . . .

TANKY: I'd like to go but I can't leave Chalky.

The HEROES *assemble upstage in heroic positions ready for battle and form a tableau.*

DINGO: That's not Chalky.

TANKY: It is Chalky.

DINGO: No it's not. Look, look out there. You see faces . . . ladies . . .

TANKY: They've come to see Chalky and me being brave.

DINGO: No.

TANKY: Evening.

DINGO: No. Mothers down there. And wives and daughters and sisters . . . roger so far?

TANKY: Roger . . . and I want to thank you all for being such a wonderful audience to play to . . .

DINGO: Mothers. Seen their sons go off with lust and blood in their eyes – mud on their boots . . . you know what? They used to wave the boats off.

TANKY: Really – I want you to know from the bottom of my heart . . . it's been a privilege to play to you tonight. Stop on, you'll hear some lovely singing.

DINGO: Used to wave the boats off full of waving sons – husbands, father, brothers, doing positive and constructive work . . . roger so far?

TANKY: Roger – as one of our finest soldiers said he said 'man does not live by bread alone.'

DINGO: They're up there watching.

TANKY: Mothers.

DINGO: Yes.

TANKY: Say hello, Chalky.

DINGO: No, it's grotesque – and it's not Chalky. Do you think we'd make a mistake like that? Do you think that black, burnt up, high in the sun stinking charred old toothy old jerk of raw material is a British swaddie do you? Do you think we'd risk offending offending every mother here tonight with unlikely looking material. Highly upset they'd be. That's enemy. People out there lost their dear ones – that's enemy. No British soldier dies like that. That's enemy. You won't find a photographer, a statue, a painting of a British soldier like that.

TANKY: He died well, did Chalky.

DINGO: That Chalky? Never. they would not have it. They'd be up in arms if they thought that was a killed on the field of honour green. Cross their legs and shout no more.

TANKY: He died to rid the world of evil – what about the concentration camps?

DINGO: We don't know about those yet.

TANKY: What about the Jews?

DINGO: We don't know about the Jews yet.

TANKY: He died for spiritual purpose.

DINGO: I heard him. Gott mit uns.

TANKY: He died for . . . he died anyway.

DINGO: Yes he died. He died because he couldn't get out. You've been taken in . . . that, not like that did he die. Evil enemy die like that. You've been taken in . . . like Mickey Mogg there panting to join the colours. He' just taken in . . . because he hasn't done it.

What you have there is a Kraut . . . you can tell by his brutal chin.

TANKY: Uuuuuuuugh. Bloody Kraut.

He throws CHALKY *away in disgust . . . as he does the* HERO COLONEL *drops raised hand, and bagpipes, smoke, barrage 'Alamein'. The* COMIC *catches* CHALKY *and tucks him under his arm.*

DINGO: The best place to be in a battle is in the thick of it, only with your head down and a look of eager blood-lust in your eyes. Better still if you look confident you know where you are, you can direct others where you're not. Time spent in recce is never wasted!

They follow the others, led by the HERO COLONEL, *pistol in hand; the file of men threads its way through gunfire, and smoke and the music of Elgar. When the tumult dies, and some of the smoke clears, the* COMIC *says:*

COMIC: What can I say after that eh? (*Goes over to the* HERO SCOT.) Hello. The second battle of Alamein was a political battle you know, Churchill wanted an all-British victory before the Americans came in, did you know that it was political, it need never have been fought, I don't suppose you're old enough to vote? Do you mind if I try to cheer you up with a little story? No? Well, you've heard it like you've heard most of them before, still goes down well, though, usually – only when you laugh? Yes. Have you ever had your eyes checked? No, they've always been brown. Now, did you hear the one about the wee Jock who inadvertently stood on an S-mine? On his way back to the R.A.P. holding his bloody piece in his hands he met his Colonel who said 'I'll stop this self-abuse.' No? Only when you laugh.

The HERO SCOT *laughs, coughs blood and dies.*
Blackout. House lights up. A newsreel. Princess Elizabeth. Glenn Miller. White Cliffs of Dover.

ACT TWO

A prison camp. For other ranks, British. DINGO *and* TANKY *are here. They are here somewhere in the looping lethal wire. The wire is on frames dropped in and gets smaller and tighter as it recedes up stage. So that the effect is of barbed wire stretching, sometimes fiddle-string taut and sometimes looping in characteristic twirls – as far as the eye of a prisoner can see. There is room between the frames for movement. Searchlights pluck the wires and the wind makes the sound. The searchlights converge on an open space downstage and go out one by one. Until a small bulb dangling centre of the light circle, that will be – is switched on and in the weak diffusion of light we see* TANKY *and* DINGO. *In ragged uniform and greatcoats. And in a small boxing ring.* DINGO *and* TANKY *stand together holding hands – when they start talking they walk round in ever-increasing circles. But they start standing still.*

DINGO: In a cell.

TANKY: And me – I'm in a cell.

DINGO: In a room.

TANKY: And me – I'm in this room.

DINGO: Are you going to repeat everything?

TANKY: I'm excited. (*And he blinks excited – making faces for laughs.*) It's the first time I've been captured.

DINGO: If you're going to repeat everything I say – this cell is going to get overcrowded.

They start walking round.

TANKY: What I like is the peace.

DINGO: If you go on like that my eardrums will give away.

TANKY: And the quiet and the time to do nothing.

DINGO: Not to mention the overheating.

They pass and DINGO *pushes* TANKY.

TANKY: Don't.

They stop and look at each other. Grinning happily.

DINGO: I will if you make the room mess or whatever overcrowded.

TANKY: I won't.

DINGO: See you don't. (*Round again.*) This room is wooden stout construction from timbers from the Black Forest hard as a very hard prussian blue. Steel. And locked at night by a padlock made in Sheffield that used to clop in the hasp of tank side bin perhaps or rum ration cupboard. Strong.

TANKY: They have a bit of trouble opening it in the morning.

DINGO: A difficult padlock that often doesn't open first go.

TANKY: Wants some oil.

They lean back on the ropes arms outside.

DINGO: It's had some from the black on it.

TANKY: Good oil.

DINGO: It is good oil.

TANKY: They shouldn't waste good oil on us.

DINGO: What it is – it's bag happy like us.

They start round again coming inwards and tighter and faster as TANKY *gets a little frightened.*

TANKY: I'm bomb happy and bag happy.

DINGO: Dogs – listen! (*They stop and listen. A dog howls – and it makes* TANKY *shiver.*) Dogs – big, black and barking Adolf Hitler.

TANKY: Outside – they're outside.

DINGO: Pad round the room hut mess or whatever.

TANKY: They are outside.

DINGO: I think that's clear enough.

TANKY: Yes.

DINGO: They wouldn't be inside.

TANKY: Are they not trained?

DINGO: Of course they're trained – highly trained – best trained dogs in the world are on a German leash.

TANKY: That's all right then – they can come in then. (*Brave.*)

DINGO: Trained to kill.

TANKY: Outside. (*They stand close together holding hands.*) I thought we'd left all that – there. I thought we'd finished with all that.

DINGO: Outside.

TANKY: Highly trained.

DINGO: To kill kriegies.

TANKY: Oh well.

Relief. They start winding out again.

DINGO: You're a kriegie.

TANKY *stops.*

TANKY: When I was a nip nobbly knees that couldn't pass a wall without drawing blood from scuffed skin – and elbows . . . were you like that? I was. When I was a nip fishing in grates and drains thinking it was all water so . . . did you think that? I did. A dog bit my cheek after I furred him ever so gentle, a scottie and he wouldn't let go. I'm a kriegie.

TANKY *walks round again* – DINGO *has stopped walking.*

DINGO: It's a nickname – helps us English to reduce it to its proper size . . . minimizes the position like bomb happy does – you could laugh about bomb happy and forget how they sit and they shit . . . their trousers. Shows you're not alone – coined by the officers but filtered down.

TANKY: I'm a bloody kriegie.

They go round holding hands.

DINGO: In a cell. I said at the time name, rank and number and regiment and how many rounds I had in my rifle and morale was pisspoor. And the password was 'Tooting' and the countersign was BEC.

TANKY: Ooh 'eck. I said it was Liverpool Street.

DINGO: No matter – bloke next door said nothing and look what happened to him . . . his trouble was he looked intelligent and a gentleman.

TANKY: They don't know much do they?

DINGO: Didn't see how he could be only a trooper name rank and number and the King is at Buckingham Palace. (*On the ropes again – arms expansive and very free . . . their gestures give the lie to the words.*) Last to have a shelter. And always prepared to fight his own battles. In the bag. In the bag Tanky. (*With great delight. They embrace.*)

TANKY: In a camp.

DINGO: Round this camp have you seen? Round this camp – next time take it in – round this camp there's barbed wire.

TANKY: I've seen it.

DINGO: Doubled up.

TANKY: Waste of good wire. I see it coming in and going out.

DINGO: With machine guns winking black-eyed – from those towers – swinging winking pushing a black finger between my shoulders.

TANKY: I don't like going out.

DINGO: It's all right.

TANKY: I like the woods – but I don't like going out . . . and the dogs watching us. They ought to know we're not going to . . .

DINGO: It's a lovely justification. I wish they had a few more guards . . . young sprightly lads who could grab my ankle should I falter.

They are close together again now. A pause.

TANKY: Brighton. (*He shivers.*) Cold now – and Worthing stinks from the fish on the beach and there's that camp I'd be in – waiting . . . waiting for the invasion. (*Outside a dog howls again.* TANKY *clutches* DINGO.) You could never hope to get outside. Outside – there's these dogs trained to kill legs and throats – at your face . . .

DINGO: Outside there's a war on. Inside – I'm taking up surgery.

TANKY: And I'm taking up nothing.

DINGO: You can be two's up. (*He takes a thick volume from the inside of his greatcoat.*)

TANKY: How long does it take to be a surgeon

DINGO *flicks through the book and looks at the last page number.*

DINGO: Taking everything into consideration and the fact that they've only just given the Home Guard rifles – I'm a slow reader.

TANKY: They get good money don't they?

DINGO: No – they do it for love and the hope that they might be the very first Home Guard Field Marshal . . . L.D.V. and scar.

TANKY: I'm doing long-distance lorry driving.

They sit back to back and DINGO *reads his book.* TANKY *drives his long-distance lorry.*

DINGO: And sod-all ambition.

TANKY: Heavy goods – change up.

DINGO: When you reflect on it – there are few occupations soldiering fits you to do.

TANKY: Long-distance lorry driving.

DINGO: That's one – and there's digging. Who wants to be a digger all his life? Don't be a digger all your life. Take a day off to dig your own grave. (*An intense aside – vehement but soft, like the lucid phase of a fever.* TANKY *doesn't notice the quickening. He wipes his windscreen.*) I'll not dig my own grave . . . dig his first. I'll die screaming the more I slip – my fingers barbs – hooks . . . fish bones in the throat of death. Still when I'm cold, gob fresh shut and tied round my best shave ever, blood and spunk lead in a pencil – pennies on my eyes, still will I scream.

TANKY: Long-distance coaches – charas.

DINGO: That's one – and there's ghosting. There's always ghosting for those that soldier on and end their soldiering in the time-honoured way. Should I be a ghost – and I will be with all my tight holding on, shouldn't be a bit surprised . . . I'll make sure I do my ghosting in the sand table rooms of Sandhurst. Do you hear? Sir?

TANKY: Change down.

DINGO: I'll be there. Whenever there's a Tactical Exercise without Troops – I'll stand in for the blood and snot. I'll be there – twirling in the air behind them. Plot a move to that finger-ridged hill of sand where the sponge trees shiver. One troop up one tank up one head up out of the rattling ronson* – twirling on the vane sight I'll whisper 'k' you darling – should have died in my wanker by rights'.
We'll do it yet Tanky. (*Eyes up to heaven.*) He might – if he don't get caught, but I would not give a little boy's knot for his chance.

TANKY: We'll be there.

DINGO: Long-distance lorry driving.

TANKY: Too true – heavy goods.

DINGO: There's that – and there's just two more. Before the war – I brought up my ring to tongue my toes at the sight of sparrow raked by a cat . . . mention maternity whilst eating and I'd peck at my food.

TANKY: I'm like that.

DINGO: Still? Stick to driving. With me – the sights I've seen – the indifferentism – the dull in my head for red on my boots and what you might step on in the night . . . the normalcy of mates cut to chunks – stands me in good stead. In very good stead. I think of the two I've done right to settle for surgeon.

TANKY: You've chosen a good career there.

DINGO: Bloke at school took up butchering – took his thumb right off and he snuffed it – blood took poison.

*Tank

TANKY: Ackers in that you know.

DINGO: I think I've done the right thing to opt for surgery.

TANKY: Get the right tuition.

DINGO: It's all in here.

TANKY: If I could have gone on driving. (*They get up.* DINGO *reads his book.*) Two's up on the book then. There's no books you can get on long-distance lorry driving.

DINGO: You could get a manual.

TANKY: I could go over the roads. I told them I wanted driving – their remark to me in reply was they wasn't running the war for me lad . . .

DINGO: Who then?

TANKY: Not you then?

DINGO: Not me.

TANKY: Nor me. They told me. If they're not running it for me or thee . . .

DINGO: Stands to reason they're not running it for them.

TANKY: Who?

DINGO: You've seen them.

They stand cold still. And they listen and look at the wire – the wind flutters some striped shreds. And a dog howls again.

TANKY: Why?

DINGO: I'd run a war for them – I'd run the hardest war of all for them. I might even . . . in a cell.

Scraping underneath.

TANKY: What's that?

DINGO: In a cell . . .

TANKY: Underneath.

DINGO: Don't hear it. Nothing – don't want to hear it.

TANKY: Unless it's the dogs.

Scraping stops.

DINGO: I'm in a room.

TANKY: And me – in this room.

DINGO: In this hut.

TANKY: Hut.

DINGO: Block.

TANKY: Block.

They're getting happier as they get nearer the ropes.

DINGO: Stalag.

TANKY: Stalag.

DINGO: Enemy country.

TANKY: Enemy.

DINGO: Antagonistic populace.

TANKY: Yes.

DINGO: Why don't speak the language.

TANKY: No.

DINGO: What's more – no signposts.

TANKY: What's more – no signposts.

Expansive, arms out happiness.

DINGO: You could get lost out there.

TANKY: You could get very lost out there.

They come together and hug each other.

BOTH: You could get very lost out there.

DINGO: You know – over the years – before I qualify for my finals as a surgeon – you are going to get on my wick already raw.

TANKY: I'll try not to. I'll try not to – not to . . . (*Like a bird he begins to flutter.*)

DINGO: Bloke I know is studying engineering by the light from his little lamp.

TANKY: Those little lamps. (*But tries to hold himself down. Scraping starts again.*) Listen.

DINGO: Escaping. (*He puts his ear down to the ground.*) In a tunnel.

TANKY: Bloody fools. (*Pushes himself against the rope.*) They'll be back – you'll be back.

DINGO: Where are you going then?

TANKY: Don't know when they're well off. (*Throws himself a bit harder at *the ropes.*)

DINGO: Shall I thump the top and put the shits up them? Shall I bang so that the ceiling comes closer and little lamps flutter . . . so they think it's a Jerry . . . Achtung!

He does with his fists – a frenzy of thumps and up on his feet. Scraping stops. TANKY *throws himself hard at the ropes and bounces back to sit on his arse legs out.*

TANKY: Talking of Jerries – they've got some lovely roads for long-distance. Miles you can go.

DINGO (*leans over the ropes conversationally*): Those little lamps are rather intriguing – it might be worth explaining those little lamps to put you clearly in the picture.

TANKY: Here. Collection. (*Leans over at* DINGO's *right.*)

DINGO: Do you mind letting me tell them about the little lamps?

TANKY: No – you can tell them about the little lamps we prisoners of war make . . . tell them.

DINGO: What are you holding your hat out for.

TANKY: I think they might find it rather intriguing.

DINGO: What you do – is you take some margarine.

TANKY: The Russians don't get enough to at. (*Hurries to lean over at* DINGO's *left.*)

DINGO: And a klim tin.

TANKY: There's a collection for the Russians. (*Back on the right.*)

DINGO: Plenty of margarine. Why didn't you tell me – you could have had my margarine . . .

TANKY: Oh – I didn't know.

DINGO: Now I've been and rendered it down . . .

TANKY (*on* DINGO's *left*): That's good – I'm terrified of the dark.

DINGO: For one of those little intriguing lamps.

TANKY: For when the lights go.

He is suddenly active and throws himself at the front ropes again as the lights go off. Lands in a curled-up ball – whimpering. His hands pulling his head down back into the solid of his curled tight body. DINGO *goes spare. Leaps over the ropes and stamps and rails at the switcher off of the light.*

DINGO: That's sheer bloody mindedness – you're being a sheer bloody mind – you . . .

TANKY: Light your little lamp.

DINGO: I can't light my little lamp.

TANKY: Light your little ingenious lamp.

DINGO: I can't light my little bloody lamp. I haven't got a little twatting lamp.

TANKY: Why?

DINGO: Because. (*Searchlights flick.*) See they've got light for that. Sheer hard Kraut bloody mindedness – that and the white stinking cabbage . . . and the bread and the soup – sheer bloody bosche bloody mindlessness. Fuck the Common Market.

TANKY: I'm dark. I'm cold. Where's your little lamp?

DINGO: Where? I gave my little lamp to the Russians.

TANKY: What you do that for?

DINGO: For them to eat.

TANKY: Sheer bloody useless – let them eat their own lamps. (*He's up and straight for the ropes. But he stops and just touches them before rolling up again in a ball and whimpering.*) I can't see to drive.

DINGO: Let me feel you for surgery. (*He starts to climb back in.*)

Blackout.

Scene Two

The Bloody Beaches of Normandy.
A front cloth which is a badly-drawn map of the European theatre of war. 'The Bloody Beaches of Normandy' on the

map is lit by a spot. Enter the COMIC *in battledress and battle order, with his trousers rolled up and feet bare, carrying his shoes in his hand. The sound of seaside sea. The* COMIC *sits on the beaches and lets the head he has on him loll and shake and be all his parts in turn. His seat is on* MOGG *who lies motionless as if dead.*

COMIC: Get off my shoulders.
My head.
My head says, what does my head say, how many are dead does it say . . . what is dead to my head? What?
There is no dead – there is nothing dead, I have them up and walking.
All the lovely soldier boys.
Good luck to each one of you and good hunting on the mainland of Europe.
We mothers must grin and bear it.
It is becoming increasingly difficult to grin.
Watch my other head. My other head is horrible, that's the head to watch . . . don't watch his head . . . this head will say:
As a mother who is lying ill with Cancer and whose two boys are serving overseas, I feel I must write to express my deep appreciation of the splendid arrangements that were made for the boys from B.L.A.
No wonder the armies in your command are proved invincible in this war. Your men are treated like human beings . . .
Let no man surrender as long as he is wounded and can fight.
Do your sailors sing? In that case we will sing 'Onward Christian Soldiers'.

MOGG: Are you talking to me?

COMIC: I am talking to me.

MOGG: There is a bloke here who hits all officers.

COMIC: I'm his mother. Can I see him?

MOGG: He's being repaired.

COMIC: My great passion in life is to see things being repaired as this is so much more interesting than seeing them whole. Totally mauled, all mauled, all totally mauled around here. This would be a great place for my cheery old friend Sir Herbert Barker – bone setter . . . how many healthy active people there are in Britain today who would still be cripples or in constant pain, but for Sir Herbert Barker's wonderful gift. Now what have we here walking down yon country lane? Baaaaaaaaaaaaaaaa-aaaaaaaaaa. The spectacle of wounded and terrified animals on the battlefield is in some ways the most pathetic sight of all, woof woof, down boy, are you looking for master . . . ? Mooooooooooooo, Moooooooooooo, old girl, do you want a milkies? The memory of that moo haunts me still, advance and retreat allow no time for milking. Baaaaaaaaaaaa, baaaaaaaaaa, it was in a farmyard in an area Jerry was still disputing with us that I saw the little lamb . . . clear orf matey . . . we all know that both dogs and horses hate being watched while they eat, possibly the British soldier feels the same way about it . . .

MOGG: Sir – may I retire?

COMIC: Why?

MOGG: Sir, I have been hit three times.

COMIC: I have not touched you.

MOGG: Sir – you are sitting on me.

COMIC: How proud your mother will be to learn this.

MOGG: Sir. I would like to give you a testimonial . . . may I write you a letter?

COMIC: You may. Write it now. (*Sits on* MOGG's *knee.*)

MOGG: Sir. A man of discipline and orderly mind, you nevertheless enjoy the odder, more fantastic side of war – a strict man, you are no sober sides, you have captured the imagination of the world, not only because of your ability as a soldier but because you bring to modern times the spirit of medieval wars, when fighting was romantic and glorious . . .

COMIC: That is quite amazing because I've got a very funny face . . .

MOGG: I am grateful to have been of your army . . . I am sir, your obedient servant 14417695 Private Mogg. M. I

I can smell them . . . there are Germans.

COMIC: Now then; that smacks of belly-aching to me, I would be the first to be informed if there were Germans about . . . you are a very fine and dutiful armchair of a private soldier and I am glad I have got you, but you are not fully in the picture, you are concerned with grains of sand, you are seeing trees where you should see woods, you would make an excellent Sergeant Major of Pioneers but you would never make a General . . . today we will fight the battle of Normandy and it will be terrific, terrific, I looked over the ground with a fine tooth comb before I sat down on you . . . if there are Germans within two hundred yards I should be very surprised and dead as I expected you to be with all these poor boys lying around . . .

MOGG: But I am not dead. If I point the Germans out to you, will you make me a Sergeant Major?

COMIC: I will, I will do more, I will let you wear my funny hat.

Blackout.

Scene Three

A prison camp. MOGG *stands downstage left in a searchlight beam. He is dressed as a Sergeant Major and a Hero and very smart. A hint of stained glass in his uniform. The searchlight beam is used as a follow spot.* TANKY *is in the ring huddled up in the far corner.* DINGO *is half over the ropes and half not. When* MOGG *appears he says one leg over for a few speeches.*

MOGG: In the field.

TANKY: Don't hit me.

DINGO: What?

MOGG: In the field – sergeant major in the field.

DINGO: It means nothing to me.

TANKY: Have you got a little lamp.

MOGG: I got promoted to sergeant major in the field.

DINGO: You can't have surgery. I bagged surgery weeks ago, didn't I Tanky? There's only one book – come out from your womb Tanky and tell him – back me up. You haven't got the intelligence anyway.

TANKY: Light my darkness. (*It's cold.*)

MOGG: Who's senior soldier.

DINGO: Who opened the gate?

MOGG: Who's in command?

DINGO: Who let you in?

MOGG: In the field for bravery I was promoted to sergeant major and I would have gone on to do great things in the field.

DINGO: Looking for a field sir?

TANKY: It's cold.

DINGO: There's a wind up your back. It's come from the plains of Siberia . . .

MOGG: I've found a field.

DINGO: . . . from the parade ground of Catterick. Should you be looking for a field – I know of a field . . .

MOGG: I've found it.

DINGO: You'll be all right then sir. Only – if it doesn't turn out right sir . . . you might like to try a wider field – turn right at the shithouse, figures two hundred yards till you get to the wire then trip it . . .

MOGG: I know you.

DINGO: I know you.

TANKY: I'm starved – born in a field?

DINGO: I'm cold too.

MOGG: I should think you are.

DINGO: Well – I'll tell you. How are we with the Commandant . . . that's how we are. (*Two fingers crossed under* MOGG's *nose.*) And that's him on top. Chuffed. And that's us underneath – chuffed highly.

TANKY: Old Dot and Carry One.

DINGO: That's him.

TANKY: That's him – he's all right.

DINGO: On top – and that's us underneath and I'm studying surgery . . .

TANKY: And I'm doing long-distance lorry driving.

DINGO: When I'm not working on agriculture in a supervisory capacity because I'm a lance corporal . . .

TANKY: He supervises me.

DINGO: I put myself on orders. Next week I'm going to be a sergeant. (*He chalks a stripe on his uniform sleeve.*)

MOGG: I find you disgusting.

DINGO: You find us chuffed.

MOGG: I find you collaborating.

DINGO: You find us living.

TANKY: We only chop trees.

DINGO: Geneva says work – and non-commissioned officers in a supervisory capacity. That's me.

MOGG: King's Rules and Regs say escape. And harry – and tie them down to running after you – and keep the manpower tight and concentrated on watching you.

DINGO: They do. Listen. (*Clambers into the ring.*) Under here. Under my feet as I talk to you now there's officers struggling like blacks and scraping away the very earth from under our very feet. There's a dienst* on. But not us – officers only . . . like pissups all night and resigning. It's the way they're brought up. We can't fit it in – what with Geneva convention graft and studying for a surgeon – we don't have the energy for it.

TANKY: I've hurt my back.

DINGO: He's not well for escaping – and I get terrible claustrophobia in tunnels and wooden horses. Don't I?

TANKY: All I want is some light.

DINGO: Can you just move over to the edge of your heroic light that you've no doubt earned in the field . . .

MOGG: For single-handed . . .

DINGO: Yes – can you stand so it tips some over my mate.

*An Escape.

MOGG *motions for* DINGO *to help him into the ring. Rude refusal.* MOGG *stands by* TANKY.

MOGG: Get up . . . you disgust me.

DINGO: Get up . . . you disgust him.

TANKY *rises in the air and slides down as a hole in the ground is opened. A figure comes out – just head and shoulders. The* NAVIGATING OFFICER *that we last saw in the desert going over the top gloriously is now escaping gloriously. At least – his head and shoulders are.*

NAVIGATING OFFICER: I'm a British Officer.

MOGG *leaps to attention and flings him one up.*

MOGG: Sir!

NAVIGATING OFFICER: This is Coblitz.

MOGG: Sir.

DINGO: No Sir. If you want Coblitz – that's outside the wire in Westphalia about two or six kilometres this side of Munster . . .

NAVIGATING OFFICER: I'm an escaping Navigating Officer. I know you.

DINGO: I know you.

NAVIGATING OFFICER: I know Coblitz when I see it. Cave! (*Bobs down and is gone.*)

MOGG: Did you see that?

DINGO: Very impressive.

MOGG: Did you see that – you louse-bound defeatist?

He kicks TANKY *hard* – TANKY *curls up tighter.*

TANKY: Ooooooooooooo. That hurt.

MOGG: Get to your feet – on your feet where an Officer's been. You disgust me.

DINGO: You disgust him Tanky.

MOGG: And you – you make me want to throw up.

DINGO: Well – you know what I'm like – sick-making.

MOGG: Up. (*Another kick.*)

TANKY: You can't make me. I can't get up – it's the dark.

DINGO: It's not that dark.

TANKY: I have the horror of the dark – tell him.

MOGG *kicks* TANKY *again.*

MOGG: Where's your head – let's see your head for my boot – I want to kick your head.

DINGO: He doesn't like the dark – not since he nearly died in the dark.

TANKY: I couldn't get out of this tank – oooh that hurt – you're hurting. I have to sleep near the window . . .

MOGG: When I've finished with you you'll want to escape – when I've finished with you – you'll be over the wire like a lot of happy harriers – you'll beg me to shove you up a tunnel. Come out – till I stamp on your head.

TANKY: Hey . . . that hurt again.

MOGG: Do you see?

DINGO: I see.

MOGG: As an example that's all.

TANKY: Tell him to jack it in.

DINGO: He won't Tanky – he's found his field.

MOGG: The sooner you bring out your head – the sooner you'll see some light.

The light is switched on again. And TANKY *looks out. He looks at* MOGG *and curls up again. He beats the floor.*

TANKY: I thought we'd finished with that, there's always something else . . .

MOGG: Come out.

DINGO: He doesn't like officers either – not since he nearly died from associating with an officer.

MOGG: I'm not an officer.

DINGO: Keep sweating.

MOGG: I'm proud of my rank – promoted in the field.

DINGO: In his state – you're all the same. And you're a hero – but he doesn't like heroes either.

TANKY: Not since a hero nearly stuck his bayonet in my tummy. Once.

MOGG: You're a collaborating shagnasty – what are you?

TANKY: Oooooooooooh.

DINGO: You're going to make this Stalag the smartest best Stalag in enemy-occupied whatever . . .

MOGG: Right. What are you?

TANKY: A collaborating . . . sir.

MOGG: A collaborating what?

TANKY: Yes.

MOGG: Where's your head – bring your head out till I open it. Where is it?

TANKY: Oooooooooh.

DINGO: You've found your field then? Who's on outside area?

MOGG *looks at* DINGO *and thinks – at the same time he kicks* TANKY *hard absent-mindedly but hard on the end of every question regardless of whether* TANKY *answers or not.*

MOGG: The outside area is zift. What is it?

TANKY: Ooooooooh – zift . . .

MOGG: Sir.

TANKY: I was going to say that sir. Sir.

DINGO: All the stones want dressing off.

MOGG: Wants to look something like – what does it want to look like Tanky?

TANKY: Something like – sir.

DINGO: Morale will soar.

MOGG: You see because morale is slack.

TANKY: Slack sir.

MOGG: Don't anticipate the word of command – right?

TANKY: Right – ooooooh.

DINGO: Sitting still in a prison camp is a legal offence in the military sense – or being in possession of the mind and purpose to sit still and go white in the head, likewise, but more difficult to prove. And because it's an offence – it can in no way be condoned.

WILLIE *sits beside him. He is a big soft lovable guard with lots of photographs of his children and his Frau in his inside pocket. He hunts for them now. Hands his rifle to* DINGO *while he does it.*

MOGG: Morale is shot to buggery – what is it?

TANKY: Shot. It's shot.

MOGG: What?

TANKY: Shot.

MOGG: To what?

TANKY: Shot sir – shot sir.

MOGG: I'll say it again son so that you can digest it, learn and inwardly digest. Morale is shot to buggery – what is it?

TANKY: Ooooooooo. Morale see – when I were a nip with nowt but a love of Jesus and I did love him I expected all the time for him to look after me – when't lads used to make me roar gi'ing me Indian burns and ear rubs I used to cry to Jesus at fost – then I didn't do owt . . .

MOGG: Stop stop talking in the ranks – show us your head – bring it out so I can kick it.

DINGO: Is this your frau then Willie? I bet she belts like a little rattlesnake eh? I think she's very nice – sehr gut.

TANKY: It wor only cos of my big head – and t'way I used to talk then . . . I used to talk like they talk in Derbyshire . . . that's where I come from . . . Jesus. Dingo . . . Dingooooooooooooooooooooooooooo.

TANKY *jerks out straight and tries to get up* – MOGG *kicks him hard on the head and he goes down like a stone.*

DINGO: These your chickoes then Willie? I bet you have merry adam with them – he's a real little monkey isn't he? I think they're very nice – schone.

MOGG *kicks* TANKY's *head again and again so it gets beaten to a jelly.*

WILLIE: Feldwebel nicht? (*A nod at* MOGG.)

DINGO: That's it.

WILLIE: Ja ja.

DINGO: His career was cut short in the field of battle just when he was about to make a name for himself – he's going to make this the smartest Stalag in wherever.

WILLIE: Ja ja.

DINGO: He's persuading Tanky to escape.

WILLIE: Ja – gut.

DINGO: He's already persuaded me. I intend to escape in full view.

WILLIE: For you – the war is over – nicht?

DINGO: I thought so Willie.

WILLIE: Ho ho – sehr gut.

DINGO: Tanky.

MOGG: That's better.

DINGO: Tanky's never been the same since he lost his mate.

MOGG *leans over the rope – breathing hard.*

DINGO: Breathing heavy?

MOGG: It's a bit embarrassing. (*He adjusts his dress.*)

The COMIC *enters carrying little lamps. He is accompanied by a group of giggling* GIRLS. *Three almost identical girls in long blonde wigs and dressing-gowns. They set up the booth.*

COMIC: Stand up when the Commandant arrives – normal courtesy.

MOGG: I suppose it was the excitement.

DINGO: I'm escaping – I'm bribing a guard – this one here . . . he's going to swap clothes and places and he'll be a kriegie and I'll be a goon – He'll munch Red Cross all day long and study accountancy – and I'll chew sausage and belt holy seven colours out of the Russians – that right Willie.

MOGG: I shot my lot. He was a despicable.

DINGO: You've persuaded me.

MOGG *notices* WILLIE *for the first time. He recovers his breath and yells.*

MOGG: Goon in the block.

DINGO: Where?

COMIC: Goon in the block.

DINGO: Goon in the block?

WILLIE *looks embarrassed and shifts from one foot to another.* DINGO *still holds his rifle and bayonet.*

GIRLS: Goon in the block. (*They pop their heads round the proscenium.*)

DINGO: Oh – you mean Willie? Yes. Goon in the block.

TANKY *gets up and staggers towards the ropes. The* COMIC *waits tense and* DINGO *crouches down.* MOGG *stands well back from* TANKY *as the lights go out and a searchlight flicks. A dog howls.*

TANKY: When I was a nip nobbly knees I smoothed the coat of this rough-haired terrier . . .

As he reaches the ropes the lights go out, searchlights flick and a klaxon sounds. He gets to his feet in the glare of the searchlight and staggers a bit. Then rushes the rope – bounces off. A great Ooooooooooooooooooh of real disappointment goes up from all assembled. He tries again. And again. And again. And again – hangs over. WILLIE *stands underneath and pushes his bayonet into* TANKY's *stomach and* TANKY *holds it as it goes in.*

TANKY: 'kin 'ell.

WILLIE *pulls it out red. And* TANKY *slumps on the ground grinning. Blackout. Applause from everybody as the lights go up.*

COMIC: Hard luck.

GIRLS: Hard luck.

MOGG: Good try.

DINGO: Yeah very good try.

WILLIE *has gone and* MOGG *is down outside the ring. Very chuffed.*

COMIC: Keep the first three rows for the Officers. (*In his booth introduces the Camp Concert.*) And now a big hand for those lovely leggy ladies, the Harry Titters Girls.

A group of British Officers dressed in wigs and bikinis do a fine number about 'There's something about a soldier that is fine, fine, fine'. At the end one goes down the trap.
N.B. The Camp Concert continues through to the end of the escape, and the songs and bad jokes should be improvised by the cast on the framework suggested.

COMIC: Thank you. All the world loves a Sergeant Major, and here's our own lovable one.

MOGG *marches very correctly to the centre stage. Salutes . . .*

COMIC: They tell me Sergeant Major, they tell me morale is at a very low ebb . . .

MOGG: That's right.

COMIC: What will you do?

MOGG: I'll kick their teeth in.

COMIC: What do I do. There is a code you know. (*He stands under the towering figure of the* COMMANDANT *who carries a sabre. The* COMIC *looks up at him and salutes.*) My word. My word. What do I do if a German Officer asks the way? I remember that he is bound to be twice as windy as I am because he doesn't speak the language. I stay put and I say nothing and I carry on with my job.

COMMANDANT: What is your job?

COMIC: I'm a traffic policeman.

COMMANDANT: I say . . . I am very happy to be here, to see your concert. I want you to be the first to know that I am to be transferred to the front . . . for you the war is over, for me it is just about to begin . . . I thank you, and carry on.

MOGG: Now when I first came to this camp – morale was at a very low ebb, no spirit, no get-up-and-go . . .
No . . . .
No . . . .

DINGO *walks across, very slack.*

DINGO: Hello.

MOGG: Hello what?

DINGO: Hello, what do you want? (*Stands playing the comic-unconcerned-with a fag.*)

MOGG: What do I want?

DINGO: Yes – what do you require – Jack? (*Plays to the audience of* COMIC *and* GIRLS *who lap up his mock bravado. This is the true British Squaddie. A very cheeky chappie.*)

MOGG: I've had trouble with you before haven't I?

DINGO: I shouldn't be a bit surprised. (*Large wink and large wide-swept puff on his cigarette.*) Does haircut ring a bell?

MOGG: Haircut?

DINGO: Hair – cut.

MOGG: Haircut rings several bells.

COMIC: Get your hair cut.

DINGO: Yes I thought it might – I'm the bloke you always check for a hair-cut.

MOGG: Where was it?

DINGO: El Alamein?

MOGG: Or was it Sidi Rezegh?

DINGO: It might have been – I was excused boots at Sidi Whatsit . . . or was it Wadi Whojit? (*Puts his cigarette in mouth and hands in pockets.*)

MOGG: Cold?

DINGO: No, it was very hot at Sidi Whatever.

MOGG: You got cold hands?

DINGO: Nobody's every complained before.

MOGG: Pockets.

DINGO (*tries his hands flat on his cheeks*): No. Not they're not cold – feel . . . they're not cold . . . I've kept them warm in my pockets. Feel.

MOGG: I don't want to feel your bloody hands trooper.

DINGO: Bloody speak for yourself.

COMIC: Now then. (*Annoyed. – Near the knuckle that.*)

MOGG: Pockets my lad. Are your hands so cold you've got to keep them in your pockets – there.

DINGO: Oh no – what I'm really doing is scratching my arse – sir. (*Large and engaging grin, he's lovely.*)

MOGG: I didn't ask you where your brains were . . .

DINGO: No. And I didn't tell you.

MOGG: I'll have you.

DINGO: You couldn't have relations.

MOGG: Heels.

DINGO *clicks his heels together and stands in the clasic, insolent heart of gold style beloved by our* COMIC *and the* GIRLS. MOGG *walks slowly round him.* DINGO *does a cigarette gag with his lighted cigarette like a good old cockney comic – he puts it in his closed mouth as* MOGG *walks past the front of him and then takes it out as he goes behind, puffing, eyes rolling like a good old cockney comic right and left with a grin, an inane grin like a good old cockney comic – all done with the lower lip. Someone runs on and tells a few bad jokes while the* COMIC *tries to drag* DINGO *to the trap.*

NAVIGATING OFFICER: Now I'd like to sing The Freeze Song.

A BLONDE: The Freeze Song?

NAVIGATING OFFICER: For he's a jolly good fellow . . .

DINGO: I'm not getting away up your tunnel!

COMIC (*recovering*): And now on a more serious note, a song that has kept us going through many a long and lonely hour, when the dear ones have seemed impossibly far away . . .

The BLONDES *slowly march on and with military precision lie full length on the stage.*

BLONDES: We'll all pull together . . . (*Performed as the Eton Wanking Song.*)

At the end of the song the COMMANDANT *is distracted by one* BLONDE *while one of the others slips down the trap helped by the* COMIC. *Two* BLONDES *are now left. One of them now wearing a greatcoat over his bikini sings some tear-jerking patriotic song. The* COMMANDANT *is so moved that he slowly walks to the singer, bursts into tears and caresses him. In the commotion the* NAVIGATING OFFICER *escapes down the trap. The* COMMANDANT *is in a state of emotional collapse; he is supported by* WILLIE. *The* COMIC *sets crates for the Oscar Wilde scene . . . perhaps . . . and while the* COMMANDANT *is caressing one* BLONDE, DINGO *lays hands on the other . . . the* FIRST BLONDE.

FIRST BLONDE: Let go of me. I'm an escaping British Officer.

DINGO: Give us a kiss sir.

FIRST BLONDE: Let go of me, I'm on, and I'm a British Officer.

COMIC: And now a moment of high camp drama . . .

The two BLONDES *are seated, and* MERRIMAN *enters possibly played by the* COMIC.

MERRIMAN: Shall I lay tea here as usual Miss?

CECILY (FIRST BLONDE): Yes, as usual.

MERRIMAN *exits.*

GWENDOLYN: Quite a well-kept garden this Miss Cardew.

CECILY: So glad you like it Miss Fairfax.

GWENDOLYN: I had no idea there were so many flowers in the country.

CECILY: Oh, flowers are as common here as people are in London.

GWENDOLYN: Personally I cannot understand how anybody manages to exist in the country, if anybody who is anybody does. The country always bores me to death.

GWENDOLYN, *who was the singing* BLONDE, *gets delighted applause from the* COMMANDANT *who begins to rock violently in his seat.* MERRIMAN *returns.*

CECILY: May I offer you some tea Miss Fairfax?

GWENDOLYN: Thank you. (*Aside.*) Detestable girl! But I require tea!

CECILY: Sugar?

GWENDOLYN: No, thank you, sugar is not fashionable anymore.

CECILY: Cake or bread and butter?

GWENDOLYN: Bread and butter please. Cake is rarely seen in the best houses nowadays.

CECILY: Hand that to Miss Fairfax.

MERRIMAN *does.* GWENDOLYN *tastes the tea and leaps up in annoyance and moves in the direction of the* COMMANDANT *who leans too far in his chair in an effort to poke her. He falls on his face.*

GWENDOLYN: You have filled my tea with lumps of sugar, and though I asked most distinctly for bread and butter you have given me cake . . .

COMMANDANT: Remember to pack my field service eye glass and my periscope attachment for the trenches.

WILLIE: Ja Herr Commandant.

GWENDOLYN: I am known for the gentleness of my disposition and the extraordinary sweetness of my nature, but I warn you, Miss Cardew, you may go too far.

CECILY: To save my poor innocent trusting boy from the machinations of any other girl there would be no lengths to which I would not go.

She backs into the arms of DINGO. *The* COMMANDANT *bursts into loud laughter again.*

CECILY: Let go of me. I'm a British Officer.

DINGO: I can see that by the feel of your chubby cheeks.

GWENDOLYN *escapes down the trap held by the* COMIC.

MOGG: Section Four to Forty.

FIRST BLONDE: What's section four to forty?

MOGG *hurries across to distract the* COMMANDANT.

MOGG: Offences in relation to the enemy punishable with death and buggery is one – you.

FIRST BLONDE: Oooooooh.

COMMANDANT: Remind me to have the surgeon provide me with a spare catheter, heavy duty, French wine for the passing of . . .

WILLIE: Jawohl – Herr Commandant.

MOGG: Every person who is subject to military law . . . and who on active service commits any of the following offences; that is to say . . .

COMIC *has been trying to pull the* FIRST BLONDE *to the exit, but leaves off to joke with the* COMMANDANT.

COMIC: Death.

COMMANDANT: Death. I love your Bernard Shaw.

MOGG: Without orders from his superior officers leaves the ranks . . . in order to secure prisoners, horses, or on pretence of taking wounded men to the rear . . .

FIRST BLONDE: No. Let go of me. I'm a . . .

COMIC *tries to pull the* FIRST BLONDE *to the exit.*

DINGO: I can tell that by the feel of your cottonwool bubs.

COMIC: Psst!

FIRST BLONDE: Yes.

COMIC: Now.

FIRST BLONDE: I don't want to go. I want to stay and marry him.

DINGO: I could never marry a British Officer.

COMMANDANT: Remember to pack my leather coat and my new black crop and my stomach powders and my waterproof sheet . . .

All are awaiting the FIRST BLONDE's *escape down the tunnel . . . the* COMIC *holds the exit open and grins as the* COMMANDANT *looks his way, hiding the exit with his body.*

MOGG: Having been made a prisoner of war voluntarily serves with or aids the enemy . . .

DINGO *and* FIRST BLONDE *cling to each other.*

DINGO: I don't love you darling.

FIRST BLONDE *jumps unwillingly down the exit.*

COMIC: You – er – a funny thing . . . you can say what you like about our lovable Commandant – but he's certainly got a key position in the Wermacht . . . or . . .

COMMANDANT: Sergeant – I shall want my second-best leg for the trenches and the linctus – and my leather private soldier's field equipment for my men to see I live the same conditions as them – you can carry that.

WILLIE: Jawohl – Herr Commandant. Achtung!

The FIRST BLONDE's *escape has misfired and she appears in the boxing ring. The searchlight flicks on and another joins it. She is blinded. Klaxon sounds. The* COMMANDANT *and* WILLIE *stand up.* DINGO *stands watching with his hands on his hips.* MOGG *babbles.*

MOGG: Two. By discharging firearms, drawing swords, beating drums, making signals, using words, flags, smoke, lights, or by any means whatever . . .

For a moment the sweeping lights stop on the escaping COMIC *– his foot in the trap. Klaxon pauses and in the silence . . .*

COMIC: Er . . . old Kriegies never die they simply fade away.

He bows and is gone with the light. The focus sharpens on the FIRST BLONDE *who, holding her hands over her eyes, starts to throw her spangled self at the ropes in a slow pattern build-up that begins to get frenzied as* MOGG's *speech does the same. The* COMMANDANT *draws his sabre.*

COMMANDANT: Death. Death. (*He pokes with his sabre.*)

MOGG: . . . intentionally occasions false alarms in action, on the march, or being a soldier acting as sentinel leaves his Sunray to go in search of plunder or yoni, sleeps, is pissed at his post, leaves his post without orders from his superior officer; his guard, picquet, patrol or post without being properly relieved in the field, in action, or on the march, forces a safeguard, or forces or strikes a sentinel, by word of mouth or by writing; or by making gestures or by signals spreads reports calculated to cause alarm and despondency, or does misbehave or induce others to misbehave before the enemy in such a manner as to show cowardice.

The FIRST BLONDE *throws herself at the rope and back onto the bayonet of* WILLIE *who has come up through the tunnel. She does a mincing ladylike walk to the rope alongside the dead* TANKY. *And collapses arms spread on the top rope. The* COMMANDANT *takes the blonde wig off with his sword. And he sobs. He cries.*

COMMANDANT: All my chicks have flown. I was so lenient with them – now I shall never get to the front – they are keeping me from my place in the battlefield.

WILLIE (*patting him on the back absent-mindedly*): Ja ja – gut Herr Commandant, gut. I am myself very happy. I have all the fun without being shot at, it's a soldier's dream . . .

The COMMANDANT *goes off distraught, helped by* WILLIE. *Quiet. No sound. The searchlights flick round slowly, a last time, then out.* DINGO *moves to the front of the stage and starts scraping away between his feet. He has his open book in front of him.*

MOGG: What you on?

DINGO: Escaping now, sir. (*A wailing begins.*) With the piece of bent wire – an ingenious piece of bent wire, I'm scraping my way to freedom . . . digging a shaft for my own private dienst – through sold rock under my wire.

MOGG: How long's that going to take you?

DINGO: Years. George – bleeding years, how long, that's how long . . .

MOGG: Can't have that.

DINGO: You will have that.

MOGG: I want to do my best for you.

DINGO: My duty to escape.

MOGG: That outside area is very bad. I want all those bits of paper picked up – so much paper . . . war is full of paper, have you noticed, always tossing paper around, the desert was full of paper . . . I want it all picked up and burned . . .

DINGO: Listen. (*The wailing grows louder and smoke starts to drift across the sky at the back.*) Old Dot and Carry . . . say one thing, one thing I shall say, we kept him from the front, kept him tied down so he couldn't unleash his brilliant strokes on the unsuspecting Imperial General Staff . . .

They are standing in the boxing ring now. MOGG *terrified;* DINGO *looks at him and goes over to hold his hand. It is here we see how crazed* MOGG *really is. They start the walk round the ring holding hands and* MOGG *shouting without convincing* DINGO.

MOGG: I want this to be a British camp. It shall have a guardroom.

DINGO: It shall, stand to the guard.

MOGG: Guard turn out.

DINGO: There's only me.

MOGG: And me.

They stand in the ring holding hands and listening to the wailing which gets a bit louder. MOGG *rolls his eyes and watches the black smoke drifting.*

MOGG: Black smoke means only one thing to me . . . bad cooks . . . I want this the best-organised camp wherever, right? Right?

DINGO: Right.

MOGG: Remember this is a British camp, not a rest home for hook-nosed miscreants – right? There's a lot we can do, build a theatre so we can have bum titty bum shows like the officers have . . .

DINGO: You are not having me in sequins . . .

MOGG: And a football pitch, you never thought of football pitch did you – it's for your morale . . . This go on all the time?

DINGO: What?

MOGG: Wailing, wailing . . . eh?

DINGO: That's not us.

MOGG: Who?

DINGO: That's foreign.

MOGG: I know it's foreign.

DINGO: No British kriegie goes on like that . . .

MOGG: Brace him up if he does.

DINGO: Morale – their morale is shot to buggery . . . otherwise they'd be having escapes and concerts and what a life . . .

MOGG: Goon in the block.

DINGO: They're not organised see, they've got this disadvantage, they don't take the piss out of the goons. I expect they call them guards, they don't keep on his tail, watch his funny face never knowing which way to turn, where a British Officer will pop up next . . . they need *you.*

MOGG: I'm needed here. I want this camp to be the smartest stalag this side of the Rhine . . . if we get stuck in . . .

DINGO: There's only me.

MOGG: And me. And them (*He looks at the two figures on the ropes.*) Wouldn't be so bad if they hung regular.

DINGO: And I'm escaping aren't I?

MOGG: What you think – those two?

DINGO: I think they shouldn't have joined.

MOGG: Dingo. Will you, will you, stand up for me?

DINGO: Is it for you?

MOGG: It's for you.

DINGO: I know what's for me.

MOGG: It's for me.

DINGO: Certainly. (*He stands up.*)

MOGG: Those two. On the wire, they're a bit near aren't they . . . after all- one is a British officer, which one is it?

DINGO: The one with the brassiere on. He's the British Officer.

MOGG: Will you straighten your back and get your heels together? For me.

DINGO: I might. I want you to be happy.

MOGG: Perhaps if we painted them white. (*He shoots his neck out at the two on the wire and says in his first real burst of RSM.*) Don't you let me down and you, you with the knickers on, officer or no bleeding officer . . . you loose me down by hanging irregular and I'll write Other Ranks Pisshouse on your grave. (*Now softer and like Tanky was in his cell – not a shout, but pleading.*) I'll have this stalag . . . I will call this circuit, Piccadilly Circus . . . they'll mark my words – they'll be staggered, of all the stories to come out of the Second World War this then surely is the strangest.

DINGO: Am I to stand here all day, back straight and heels together?

MOGG: I'd like you to call me sir.

DINGO: I always do, don't I sir?

The wailing stops. MOGG *sighs and adjusts himself in silence.*

MOGG: That's better. Hear myself talk.

Blackout.

Scene Four

A solo ventiloquist scene performed by the COMIC. *He sits on a lavatory. He has two puppets,* CHURCHILL *and* EISENHOWER.

COMIC: Here is a pretty pickle. The Americans want the Frankfurt area, the Ruhr, Antwerp and the line of the Rhine.

CHURCHILL: I want a battle.

COMIC: You're a very great man, Prime Minister, but you are a bit impatient.

CHURCHILL: It's high time you had another battle.

COMIC: I've had one.

CHURCHILL: I know. I heard the bells.

COMIC: I don't drink.

CHURCHILL: I want another one.

COMIC: You shall have another one.

CHURCHILL: Now.

COMIC: No. I shan't win if I have one now.

CHURCHILL: I want a battle now. I am determined to get as much fun and personal satisfaction as I possibly can out of this war and bring my rich and rousing personality to bear upon the men and women engaged in the day-to-day jobs of battle . . .

COMIC: You're always fast on our heels Prime Minister. There is only one standard of physical fitness, the standard of total war . . . we must all keep up, do you get up in the morning with a glad shout on your lips?

CHURCHILL: I get up in the morning with a bottle of white wine and a wing of chicken.

COMIC: You're a very great man.

IKE: My generals say I'm the best general the British ever had.

COMIC (*does a take and asks*): Will you say that again General? You're a thoroughly genuine person Ike . . . you really are, will you sign my autograph book before you go?

CHURCHILL: I will.

COMIC: I've got yours Prime Minister.

CHURCHILL: I want a battle now.

IKE: I agree. Let me go on to Falaise and we'll drive the British back into the sea for another Dunkirk.

CHURCHILL: Who said that?

COMIC: He's a very great and good man but he is an American . . . man, don't worry Prime Minister – we cannot come out through Dunkirk as the Germans still hold that place . . . are you full of binge? I have a master plan.

IKE: Bradley has called your plan the most imaginative of the whole war . . . but he doesn't like it.

COMIC: I don't like it. I don't like it. It's a hard nut to crack, it shall be called Market Garden and I don't like it, but I'm going to do it . . . None of us likes it.

CHURCHILL: I like it. It will gleam and flow in the annals of history. I want to see it.

COMIC: There's nothing to see.

CHURCHILL: There must be!

COMIC: No, really.

CHURCHILL: Don't try to tell me that. I was at Bull Run . . . I mean Omdurman . . .

COMIC: I wasn't. I wasn't at Dieppe and I'm not going to be at Arnhem . . . There's really nothing to see. You are a very great man but there is nothing to see, sit down and try harder . . .

CHURCHILL: Don't give me that. If there's nothing to see – why do you keep doing it.

COMIC: You keep telling me to.

CHURCHILL: That's right. Because I want to see . . .

COMIC: I don't want to see.

IKE: I agree.

COMIC: Good. You're a great man and

*This scene may be replaced by an alternative scene, from the orginal versions, see Appendix B.

a good man for an American man . . . Will you write a letter saying you completely agree and showing your wonderful humanity in your own thoroughly personal way . . . because although I would never dream of discussing such things in a lavatory, I think my plan is full of holes . . . Ahhhhhhhhhhhhhhhhhhh, Ahhhhhhhhhhhhhhhhhhhhh. Arrrrrrrhem. Arnhem. (*A silence as they contemplate – the* COMIC *then gives an apologetic little laugh.*) Dropped a large one there, didn't we . . . have you see me balance a fly whisk on one finger?

Blackout.

DOCTOR (*speaking over sounds of battle*): Where does it hurt – in the stomach – can you feel anything in your stomach son – your back, my back, your leg . . . throat, say if you feel, feel, the stump requires copious dressings and firm bandaging. Three inches above the elbow joint, wrist-conservation of the hand is of vital importance, thumbs, fingers, or parts of them must be preserved if viable, keep your head up son, blood down his throat, I told you to keep his head up, you are standing on his entrails, don't pull, for God's sake don't pull, of course he is screaming . . .

Scene Five

The camp paraded for the entry of the Victorious Allied Armies. MOGG *perks up at the sound of the coming. He leaps to his feet.* DINGO *and* WILLIE *parade.*

DINGO: I'm escaping, I'm up a tunnel, with this ingenious little spade made of klim tins and filling socks with holes in them . . .

MOGG: When I give the word of command I want to see you snap into it.

DINGO: Will I go home?

MOGG: You will, you will, I'll see to it, just you make this camp . . . here in the heart of Hitler's Germany . . . a camp that refused to recognise defeat – no goon dared put his ferret face round the abort . . .

DINGO: . . . more in fear of marching across this Sergeant Major's parade ground . . . than their own feldwebels . . . put the fear of Christ and the Russian front up them . . . For my wife who cries, don't cry . . . I'm coming home . . .

MOGG: Of all the stories to come out of the Second World War . . . (*Looks at the two bodies hanging untidily on the wire.*) . . . I'm very worried about them two . . . Still at least we look something like, stand still, Willie . . . I expect they'll make allowances.

DINGO: If they're going to worry about dressing off the caput mortum they're going to have their work cut out . . . I mean to say, with some camps . . . eh Willie?

WILLIE: We didn't know.

MOGG: Stand still and all will be forgiven.

The Liberating Music is getting louder as they wait. Standing at attention in the almost empty camp.

DINGO: My wife – it comes as a shock, I haven't thought of you once, I have thought of you once, twice, twice I've thought of you. This is . . . is it – it will be.

He tosses away his surgery. The music stops. There is nobody here but the music stops. A silence. And then . . .

NAVIGATING OFFICER: I'm a Navigating Officer. This is Coblitz.

MOGG: No. No. This is Stalag what? What?

DINGO: What?

WILLIE: We did not know.

MOGG: Or as we prefer to call it – Chipping Sodbury . . . you want Coblitz sir, you don't want Coblitz . . . have Chipping Sodbury.

NAVIGATING OFFICER: You know it's terribly buck-making to see this sort of thing.

The procession is getting nearer.

MOGG: Present arms!

The COMIC *arrives waving his hand*

and saluting, very jolly. He is accompanied by an ADC *and a bunch of* OFFICERS. *He carries* CHALKY *and says to great laughs and sniggers . . .*

COMIC: My wife. My Mother-in-law!

MOGG: Parade ready for inspection, Sir.

The COMMANDANT *has crept on in a corner, with a white flag.*

ADC: You know General, this is bloody marvellous . . . in the heart of Hitler's tottering Reich . . . like on the parade ground of Caterham . . .

MOGG: Barton Stacey actually sir, though we did our best to get our feet up. (*Carried away by the admiration of all he marches forward – with looks at everyone to make sure they are looking – and shouts at* CHALKY.) Get your *hair cut*!

NAVIGATING OFFICER: You know it's terribly buck-making to see this sort of thing.

The COMIC *goes to look at the bodies on the wire.* COMMANDANT *moves to in front of the* COMIC.

COMMANDANT: Here in the heart of Hitler's Germany . . .

ADC: Er . . . yes.

COMIC: Well?

COMMANDANT: I surrender. (*Drops to the ground.*)

COMIC: Do you, do you, well that's just not good enough is it? Go on German, go away, German man . . . you wonder no doubt why we do not smile when you wave your hands or say good morning, or I surrender, you do not like it, . . . nor do we, we are naturally friendly and forgiving people . . . it will not always be so for we are Christian forgiving people and we like to smile and be friendly. Our object is to destroy the Nazi system; it is too soon to be sure that this has been done. That is why the British soldier does not smile. Smile! (*To the assembly.*) Go away this is a time for Englishmen.

COMMANDANT: In the German race there is nothing but evil . . . follow the precepts of Comrade Stalin, stamp out the fascist beast once and for all in its lair. Use force and break the racial pride of these German women. Take them as your lawful booty. Kill. As you storm onward, kill. You gallant soldiers of the Red Army . . .

COMIC: Not quite right, but a good try, think a little harder. You're getting warmer.

COMMANDANT *exits to think.*

COMIC (*looks at the bodies on the wire*): I will lift up mine eyes unto the hills; from whence cometh help – My help cometh even from the Lord who hath made heaven and earth terrific.

The Memorial Service begins. It includes two hymns and the Solemn Remembrance of the Dead. While they stand, TANKY *says from his place on the wire.*

TANKY: He killed me.

DINGO: Who said that?

MOGG: Who said that?

TANKY: He did.

MOGG: Who said that, I'll have him, I''ll have you.

DINGO: You couldn't have black pudding.

TANKY: He killed me.

DINGO: Tanky, come over here a minute, can you spare me a minute.

He leads TANKY *from his position on the rope to downstage.*

TANKY: He killed me.

DINGO: No.

TANKY: He bloody did.

DINGO: No. Look out there.

TANKY: Ghoulish buggers . . . (*He turns away from the audience.*)

DINGO: Hey, hey, come on Tanky, you're a hero, having died . . .

TANKY: I don't hold with bleeding heroes.

DINGO: No, no, look out there, I've told you before . . . out there, mothers. You allus appeal to the mums.

TANKY: They should be home burning their kids' toys.

DINGO: No, no I look at them, we're all going home . . . and you'll be left as a cross, so have a good look . . . now then, how did he do more than his duty, eh? Willie?

TANKY: Not Willie, he's all right is Willie . . . Mogg.

DINGO: No, look – see here Tanky, if it was killing, murder, if an officer or N.C.O. does murder when he suggests they do things, when he enthuses them with the wish to please them, for the good reasons he always has . . . if that, then, would any magistrate in the land take any notice whatsoever of a gallant war record? Eh? What do you hear them all say? – eh? – Because of your gallant war record . . . because of your fine military background, eh? Now they wouldn't say that if it was murder, would they?

TANKY: He killed me.

DINGO: Look, if he killed you, if every bloke as went for a shit with a rug round him blames it on the blokes that sent him out – see my reasoning?

TANKY: He killed me.

DINGO: That would make all these public figures who directed the course of events, well, I hesitate to say it – every general colonel, corporal, will tell you how they hated doing it . . .

TANKY: Shouldn't have joined them. They all lapped it up . . . It's very interesting . . . he killed me. And they saw it.

DINGO: I can't convince him.

FIRST BLONDE: I'm a British Officer.

At the end of the service there is a long silence. And then the COMIC *puts his hand out and picks up the* FIRST BLONDE's *head. As he does so a great wailing goes up so he drops it again. The wailing stops.*

MOGG: It's all right sir, it's not him . . . I must say I was worried about him. I was going to have him painted up.

COMIC: Yes. (*He picks up the* BLONDE's *head again.*)

FIRST BLONDE: I'm a British Officer.

MOGG *who has fussed forward to deal with the situation leaps back in astonishment. There is laughter from all assembled. The* COMIC *lifts* TANKY's *head.*

TANKY: He killed me. (*At which everybody falls about again.*)

MOGG: Very good . . . very good.

FIRST BLONDE: I'm a British Officer in disguise.

COMIC: You're what? Ladies and gentlemen, and here is a British Officer . . . and how old are you.

FIRST BLONDE: Nineteen actually.

COMIC: Nineteen. (*And a big hand for the British Officer of nineteen.*) Tell me – er lieutenant?

FIRST BLONDE: Harold.

COMIC: Harold, tell me where were you captured?

FIRST BLONDE: I was put in the bag at Dieppe.

COMIC: Dieppe! (*And a big hand for the British Officer of nineteen captured at Dieppe.*) Tell me Harold before you were captured you gave a good account of yourself?

FIRST BLONDE: My men and I . . . we fought to the last man – I got twenty-five of them . . . it was a real killing match because we were determined to put up a really good show . . . I got some twenty-five I'm sure of and perhaps one or two more in the dark . . .

COMIC: Twenty-five! (*A very big hand for the British Officer of nineteen captured at Dieppe who got twenty-five of them.*) He admits to . . . (*A wink and laughter.*) Tell me Harold – you got put in the bag at Dieppe, and we learnt a lot at Dieppe . . .

DINGO: Surgery.

COMIC: . . . but you didn't stay there long did you . . . they couldn't hold you in any prison camp . . .

FIRST BLONDE: Well I was itching to get back into the scrap.

COMIC: Scrap.

FIRST BLONDE: Before the other chaps pegged more than me.

COMIC: Lucky bastards.

FIRST BLONDE: Galling not to be in at the death.

COMIC: Death.

FIRST BLONDE: So I got first reserve on a dienst, that is an escape, and hard luck the other chap caught a cold . . . and was in tears when I had to field in his place.

COMIC: Hard luck.

DINGO: Fuck his luck.

FIRST BLONDE: Concert Party actually – we were the Harry Titters Girls . . . we had a go.

COMIC: No prison camp could hold you.

FIRST BLONDE: That was the idea.

COMIC: Away – what was your route?

FIRST BLONDE: Well I got skewered on the wire actually. It hurt . . . it hurt . . . it hurt . . .

DINGO: Right up his gonga.

MOGG: We can do without that.

DINGO: Give him a big hand. (*They do.*) Right round his earhole.

COMIC: And only nineteen .. . and he came all this way to be with us today . . . isn't that just superb? Now Harold, because you're nineteen and because you're dead, and because you were gallant at Dieppe . . . I'll tell you what we'll do . . . you Harold can choose any major prize you wish without answering any questions at all. (*Applause all round.*) What's going to be . . . (*He turns the* FIRST BLONDE's *head so it whispers in his ear.*) What? No – er Harold . . . you can't have that – only the King himself can grant you that. Yes? No – er Harold . . . you cannot have the Victoria cross . . . you have chosen the one decoration it is not in my power to award. You know the rules of the show. Yes. Yes Harold – I can give you the Distinguished Service Order . . . and here it is! (*To wild applause from all except* DINGO *he drops the* FIRST BLONDE's *head and takes out a box containing a DSO. A special lining of purple satin and a gold clasp. He looks for somewhere to pin it. And turns to the* ADC *who is clapping like a Trojan.*) They usually have a little loop don't they – don't they? (*And here follows one of those delightful little official balls-ups that is so delightful and so funny. Finally he pins it to the seat of the* FIRST BLONDE's *panties. And pats it.*) You've got a nasty place there. (*Lifts* TANKY's *head.*)

TANKY: He killed me.

Wailing is heard.

COMIC: Have you all got Army Form B2626? They're all the same, so don't bother to look over each other's shoulder. This is the form you must fill in if you wish to vote in the general election. We have won the German war, let us now win the German peace.

COMMANDANT (*entering*): Might I say . . . the Socialists.

COMIC: No you may not say . . .

COMMANDANT: . . . must be beaten.

COMIC: Yes, you may say.

COMMANDANT: It must not happen. It would mean the ruin of Europe if the Socialists come to power in England.

DINGO: I'm cold. I want to go home, I'm shivering with cold – all cold all over.

COMMANDANT: I have shares in the Ruhr . . .

DINGO: Have you, have you?

COMMANDANT: And I hear that one of the plans is for the nationalisation of the mines, this is against human nature. Now is the time to work, everybody must work, managers and men, below ground and above . . . I do surrender and I'm sorry.

COMIC: Very good, you may now surrender to me, but be respectful . . .

He takes the COMMANDANT's *flag and sword.*

DINGO: Mogg, I'm cold, hug me warm . . .

For the first time he seems to be losing his grip. He sits on the floor and shivers.

CHURCHILL (*a slide*): No Socialist system can be established without some form of political police.

COMIC: You're a very great man Prime Minister, but you're going to lose the election, you are, you really are . . . (*A great burst of wailing, and the* COMIC *gets angry.*) What is that dreadful noise? You, you're a navigating officer, find out what that noise is . . . (NAVIGATING OFFICER *exits.*) . . . this is no time for belly-aching in the background.

DINGO: I'm going home . . .

COMIC *turns on* DINGO.

COMIC: For five long years the lusty youth of this great country has bled and died. (*Puts his hand on* DINGO's *head.*) Well done thou good and faithful servant.

MOGG *pushes himself under the other hand.*

MOGG: They're a lot of swindlers out for themselves, Conservative or Labour. What is the use of voting. It will not make any difference.

COMIC: My 'usband will not be at 'ome to vote. But he has told me what he wants. A good house with a bit of garden, he wants a job at a fair wage, no matter how hard the work may be, he wants a good home for his children, and educating for them. He wants to feel they won't have to go through what he went through in this war.

DINGO (*to* MOGG): Vote, vote. I am . . . I want to go home that's all there is to it.

MOGG: Did they tell you it was sexy? They told me.

More wailing. Very loud indeed.

COMIC: Will nobody rid me of that noise?

The wailing stops. The NAVIGATING OFFICER *returns. He is white as a ghost where he is not green.*

NAVIGATING OFFICER: They'll have to shoot them. A wailing mound, black holes all wailing at me. A mound of . . . people . . . all wailing and they moved. I'm a navigating officer and I'm lost.

COMIC: This is the Lord's doing and it is marvellous in our eyes. You will all go and see, you will go one by one and you will look at what has been found, one by one . . . this then is the true horror of the mansion of death . . . now there is silence. One by one, don't push.

MOGG: Come and see.

DINGO: No.

The NAVIGATING OFFICER *sits on the ground at the back and starts to sing 'Jerusalem'. The soldiers queue to see the horror of where it is: Belsen, Buchenwald, wherever.*

DINGO: I want to go home to my wife who cries, she has cried since that day I went away, she cried because I went away – she cried all the time I was in the drill hall down the road, she cried when I moved to Wembley Stadium, a twopenny bus-ride, she cried all week-end I was home, she has cried since 1939 . . . she doesn't cry because I'm shot at . . . she cries because I've gone away, and she won't stop crying and she will go out of her mind and be put in hospital for ever, which she did, which is where she is to this very day. The thing I blame that bastard for more than anything is that he has taken away my sorrow, like the lads on that bloody ridge, the first time I knew it was gone, like we tossed the Eyetie prisoners over the ledge to their death, British soldiers did this at Keren, we did . . . I did, over. That's what I blame the bastard for more than anything, chopping off, more like wearing away, rubbing down my compassion to not a thing, it is nothing. Alamein, Alamein, Alamein . . . (*'Jerusalem' ends. Wailing.*) What was wailing, it was the wailing of my wife – it was the wailing of myself, it was the wailing of all that I have seen die and it was nothing. It is such a pity this war was not fought for them . . . I might have kept my compassion, I might not have felt guilty, which I don't, because everybody will say it was fought for them. It was not. It was fought for all the usual reasons.

The COMIC *appears in the ring.*

CHURCHILL: How far is the West Wall?

COMIC: Do you wish to go to the men's room Prime Minister?

CHURCHILL: I will wait. Is this the West Wall?

COMIC: It is. There are a lot of photographers about.

CHURCHILLL: Are all my generals here?

COMIC: I'm here – your Captain.

The COMIC *faces upstage and hitches his coat for pissing.*

CHURCHILL: Gentlemen I would like to ask you all to join me in this task. Let us all urinate on the West Wall of Hitler's Germany. This is one of those operations connected with this great conflict which must not be reproduced graphically . . .

A laugh all round and a blackout.

DINGO: Am I a fool. Are we fools, that comedians are set to lead us? From where I sat I could see a childish grin of satisfaction spread all over the Prime Minister's face as he looked down at the critical moment . . .

CHURCHILL: Your freedom is in danger. Will you vote?

DINGO: Too true I shall vote. I do not . . . I have not come all this way to be pissed on twice by Mr Churchill.

Lights up over the boxing ring. Around the two bodies on the ropes, the whole cast are gathered in tableau.

TANKY: He killed me. He killed me. He killed me.

The end.

Appendix A

The following scene from the original version of *Dingo* (Act One, Scene Four) may be incorporated into the Royal Shakespeare Company version on page 64. See note on that page.

Headquarters of the German Army in the desert. ROMMEL, *with 'Lili Marlene' being sung behind the cloth by a choir. He is a fine, clean-cut German person in a leather coat.*

ROMMEL: I want petrol, I want tanks, I want water, I want food . . . (*A* BRITISH OFFICER *walks through with his hands above his head in surrender.*) . . . and I want you to salute me – the normal courtesy if you please.

BRITISH OFFICER: I am sorry General, are you, are you then the legendary Rommel . . . ?

ROMMEL: I am.

BRITISH OFFICER: Then you should know sir, that we do not salute in the British Army without we are wearing a hat, hats, we set great store by hats . . .

ROMMEL: Then I do not ask you to salute as this would be against your soldier's code, can you perhaps give me an eyes right?

BRITISH OFFICER: I can and will, except it will be an eyes left.

ROMMEL: You are losing the war because . . .

BRITISH OFFICER: . . . because we do not have a leader like you.

ROMMEL: No. This hero worship of me by the enemy must stop, I will put out an order to the effect that British troops are not to mention my name with awe, you really should not . . . should not harp on about Rommel, I am not on your side . . .

BRITISH OFFICER: I do not believe this . . .

ROMMEL: You should, you have many able Generals yourself, though I have captured a good many of them and had little soldierly chats with them all . . . for instance my tactics . . .

BRITISH OFFICER: . . . brilliant, first-rate.

ROMMEL: . . . borrowed from Wavell, and you very often beat me.

BRITISH OFFICER: Never. Your Italians yes.

ROMMEL: They are not my Italians.

BRITISH OFFICER: Are they not?

ROMMEL: They are their own Italians. Let us move a few yards to the right – I think we are going to be shelled here. (*Moves swiftly to the right leaving the* BRITISH OFFICER *standing still, his eyes left. There is an explosion where* ROMMEL *was.*) You are the living embodiment of the positive and negative qualities of the British soldier, an extraordinary braveness and toughness is combined with a rigid inability to move quickly.

BRITISH OFFICER: I owe you my life.

ROMMEL: But you did not move.

BRITISH OFFICER: I braced myself and did not go to pieces. I say good luck to you, your only fault is that you fought on the wrong side. I am proud to say that I met and fought with Rommel . . .

ROMMEL: I do not blame you for escaping, it is your duty and I would have done the same in your position.

BRITISH OFFICER: I am sure. But I do not think you could have walked as far as I did.

ROMMEL: No. I would have had more sense and borrowed a motor car . . .

BRITISH OFFICER: I do not think I would have because I cannot drive.

ROMMEL: Then I would have learned to drive.

BRITISH OFFICER: I do not think . . .

ROMMEL: You are a nuisance and I shall shoot you if you do it again.

BRITISH OFFICER: I do not think you will, even though you do have your Hitler.

ROMMEL: He is not my Hitler.

BRITISH OFFICER: I knew you would say that. My God I knew you were a tremendous person . . . such reunions we shall have.

Exit BRITISH OFFICER *hands in the air.*

Appendix B

The following scene from the original version (Act Three, Scene Two) may be substituted for Act Two, Scene Four. (See page 88).

The Camp of the Victorious Allied Army. Victorious Officers all over the shop. The COMIC *is with the* NAVIGATING OFFICER.

COMIC: What we have here, is a map of the so-called German so-called Reich. What we will do, the Victorious Allied Armies, is give this bit to the Russians, and this bit to the Americans, and this larger bit to me . . .

COMMANDANT: What about the French? (*Wandering in to surrender this minor point.*)

COMIC: The French are not our problem, they've been given Paris. I'm just a little sick and tired of this man De Gaulle following on behind, a few miles behind the troops and picking up scraps from the table . . .

COMMANDANT: If I were the Americans I would not want that bit.

COMIC: Well you are not an American man are you, you're a German man and a pretty nasty Nazi specimen of German man at that, have you ever questioned the morality of Nazism?

COMMANDANT: Yes. I came into conflict with the Nazi organisation over tennis.

COMIC: I should think you did.

COMMANDANT: I am very keen on tennis and I have always tried to play, but whenever I wanted to play there was always duty with the Hitler Youth . . . the duty was silly and I did not go, there was a lot of fuss about it, but in the end I won.

COMIC: There you see, it can be done.

COMMANDANT: If I were the Americans I would want that bit with Hamburg in it, bit.

COMIC: That is our bit. We are having that bit and I am going on, straight through all the way, see him off, the shortest road to Berlin, what the Americans will do is draw off the enemy and I shall enter Berlin wearing two hats and on a white charger, you'll do . . . (*Mounts the* COMMANDANT *who is on all fours hoping to surrender.*)

COMMANDANT: The Americans should have Berlin, they will want Berlin.

COMIC: Now the Americans should not be greedy, they have got Paris.

NAVIGATING OFFICER (*speaking with an American accent*): France is a British Baby. Says General Patton. Hi de hi!

ALL THE OFFICERS: Ho de ho!

NAVIGATING OFFICER (*as American*): Do not please ask us to keep American forces in France.

COMIC: We shall give France to the Russians.

NAVIGATING OFFICER (*still American*): We Americans must have the ports of Hamburg, Bremen and Dover. (*Mounts where the* COMIC *was. The* COMIC *is then lifted onto the* NAVIGATING OFFICER's *shoulders by two* ADCs.) I shall give a press conference. I first saw the American soldier in Sicily, I later saw him in Italy and I formed a very high opinion of him . . . I salute the brave fighting men of America, just now I am seeing a lot of them, they are winning the war for me, you thus have a picture of British troops fighting on both sides of American troops who have suffered a hard blow, a very hard blow, hard blow, the American, this is a very fine allied picture, and the Americans are very grateful for the way I have handled it, it was most interesting and they shall not have that bit. (COMIC *is lifted triumphantly along his path on the map by the* ADCs.) I shall now make a great single push to the Elbe and Berlin and enter in a blaze of glory.

NAVIGATING OFFICER: If Montgomery is put in charge Bradley said to me, I shall go home, this is one thing I cannot take, and I said I would quit with him, I said. (*He has given the* COMMANDANT *his cigar and dismounted.* COMIC *hangs disconsolately between his* ADCs *his feet off the ground.*) It is either me or Monty.

COMIC: Now then, now then, that smacks of belly-aching to me, come back here, I feel very lonely and very sad, you shall have Bremerhaven and Bremen, I am one hundred per cent behind you, I am absolutely devoted to you, we are the best of friends, it grieves me to see uncomplimentary articles about him in the British Press, he is the captain of our team, let us rally round him and so end the destructive criticism, lend a hand, and so help win the match. (*At the offer of Bremen the* NAVIGATING OFFICER *comes over and shakes hands with the* COMIC, *who now notices the* COMMANDANT *still down but smoking.*) Who are these men?

COMMANDANT: I surrender.

COMIC: You are smoking.

COMMANDANT: I am sorry.

COMIC: Who are these men? I said to them, Union Jacks flying, they came to me and I made them wait . . . and then they stood and I said to them, I didn't talk to them . . . I said to them through an interpreter, I said, who are these men, what do they want?

ADC: Who are these men, what do they want?

COMMANDANT: I surrender.

ADC: I surrender.

COMIC: Do you, do you? Well go away and come back when you really mean it. Of all the stories . . . they came to see me and they surrendered – I said . . .

ALL: Who are these men?

COMIC: Of the men who came to me, one took poison, one shot himself, and one motor accidented himself.

COMMANDANT: I surrender.

COMIC: What bit are you from?

COMMANDANT: The Russian bit.

COMIC: Then you must surrender to the Russians in their bit.

COMMANDANT: It is impossible, they are savages, they will rape me.

COMIC: You should have thought of that before you began the war, these things . . .

The Liberation March. End of Scene Two as the COMIC *with the* NAVIGATING OFFICER *gone on before, marches triumphantly at the head of his Glorious Liberating Army. They march off the stage right, to music, and in a little while come onto the catwalk of the main set where they liberate the prison camp. At the moment they are gone.*

HAS 'WASHINGTON' LEGS? & DINGO

Published to coincide with the premiere of **Has 'Washington' Legs?** at the National's Cottesloe Theatre, this double volume also includes one of Charles Wood's best known plays, **Dingo,** in the revised version performed recently by the Royal Shakespeare Company.

Has 'Washington' Legs? is a satire on the making of an epic film about the American War of Independence. Looming over the often farcical proceedings is the eccentric figure of the veteran director, John Bean (played by Albert Finney), a walking amalgam of Hollywood's hoariest myths.

Dingo, long unobtainable in print, was first staged in 1967 at the Royal Court. It is Wood's most savage and, many would say, most accomplished play.

'. . . an extraordinary occasion on which, for the first time on the British stage, one heard it suggested that the Second World War had been a bloody, sickening farce, that Churchill and Montgomery had been responsible for needless slaughter and that the compassion and humanity of the ordinary soldier had been blunted, if not erased.'

Michael Billington, *The Guardian*

'Dingo is by turns offensive, brilliant, unfair and immensely persuasive.'

Financial Times

in the same series

EAST-WEST & IS UNCLE JACK A CONFORMIST?
by Andrey Amalrik

A-A-AMERICA! & STONE
by Edward Bond

FIGHT FOR SHELTON BAR
Victoria Theatre, Stoke-on-Trent
edited by Peter Cheeseman

POOR TOM & TINA
by David Cregan

WRECKERS
by David Edgar

FROZEN ASSETS
by Barrie Keeffe

A MAD WORLD, MY MASTERS
by Barrie Keeffe

LAVENDER BLUE & NOLI ME TANGERE
by John Mackendrick

AMERICAN BUFFALO, SEXUAL PERVERSITY
IN CHICAGO & DUCK VARIATIONS
by David Mamet

STRAWBERRY FIELDS
by Stephen Poliakoff

BRIMSTONE AND TREACLE
by Dennis Potter

CLASS ENEMY
by Nigel Williams